North London Trams

Capital Transport

THE METROPOLITAN ELECTRIC TRAMWAYS COMPANY
IN MIDDLESEX AND THE NORTH LONDON SUBURBS

Robert J. Harley

First published 2008

ISBN 978-1-85414-314-3

Published by Capital Transport Publishing
PO Box 250, Harrow, Middlesex, HA3 5ZH

Printed by CT Printing Ltd

CONTENTS

4

Introduction and Acknowledgements

I arrived too late on this planet to experience at first hand the delights of riding on the Metropolitan Electric Tramways Company tramcars. My own connections to the MET come via my grandparents, who were frequent travellers on the network that once radiated out from North London into suburban Middlesex. This fine system opened its first section in July 1904 and, after almost three decades of operation, the whole company passed in the summer of 1933 to the hands of the London Passenger Transport Board (LPTB). The new owners soon adopted a comprehensive tramway abandonment policy. In a few short years, tracks were dismantled and trams scrapped.

We follow the fortunes of the Metropolitan Electric Tramways in pre LPTB days, and my narrative concludes with a brief look at the network as it existed during the trolleybus conversion period. The present volume complements my previous book on the London County Council tramways, which includes a detailed history of lines operated by the LCC, north of the Thames, adjacent to those of the MET.

When referring to the Metropolitan Electric Tramways Company, staff and passengers alike often used the acronym MET – with each letter pronounced separately. I have continued this tradition in my text.

Old issues of the *Train-Omnibus-Tram (TOT) Staff Magazine* and its London Transport successor *Pennyfare* have produced a wealth of material, especially on the social side of the organisation. The *BET Monthly Gazette* has also been consulted for information on the early years of the system. Other important reference works are listed in the Bibliography section at the end of the book.

Many people have helped in the preparation of this book. I am particularly grateful to Dr Gerald Druce, who has read through the text and has suggested suitable amendments. I also wish to record my gratitude to John Barrie, B.J. 'Curly' Cross, John Gent, Ken Glazier, Adam Gordon, Dave Jones, Terry Russell, Graham Sidwell – Editor of *Tramfare*, Rosy Thacker – former librarian at the National Tramway Museum, David Voice and James Whiting, my publisher. My late grandparents, Patricia and Alfred Little, whose stories of visits by tram to Barnet Fair and the 'Ally Pally' fascinated me as a youngster, deserve a special mention.

In this first decade of the twenty-first century almost nothing now remains of the former Metropolitan Electric Tramways Company. *Tramway Avenue N9*, listed in the London street atlas, is the last important reminder of a lost era of cheap fares and frequent, reliable services.

Heathfield, East Sussex: May 2007   Robert J. Harley

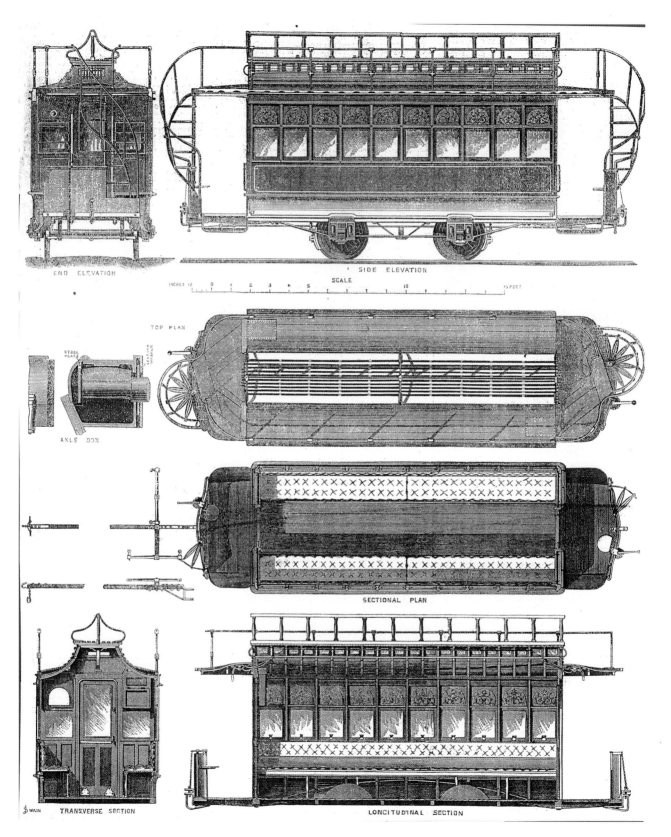

END ELEVATION

SIDE ELEVATION

SCALE

INCHES 12   0   1   2   3   4   5   10   15 FEET

TOP PLAN

STEEL PLATE

LEATHER WASHER

AXLE BOX

SECTIONAL PLAN

TRANSVERSE SECTION

SWAIN

LONGITUDINAL SECTION

6

1. Horse and Steam Power

The County of Middlesex has an interesting history. In the middle of the sixth century it encompassed the territory of the Middle Saxons, wherein lay London, the embryonic commercial and administrative centre of the nation. It was perhaps inevitable that, as London expanded, much of rural Middlesex would be gradually engulfed in a vast urban area. By 1842 one commentator recorded:

. . . one of the least counties in England, being only about 22 miles in length, and 14 in breadth. It contains 7 market towns, and about 98 parishes, without including those in London and Westminster – London is its chief place and county town. Population 1,576,636.

At the dawn of the tramway era, the author of the *1868 National Gazetteer* noted that the population had risen to just over 2,200,000 people. Amongst the working population, many of whom would use the new tramcars, we are informed that labourers' wages averaged from twelve shillings (60p) to fifteen shillings (75p) per week.

The Local Government Act of 1888 created the London County Council (LCC), thus effectively robbing Middlesex of a large slice of its administrative area. This process of territorial erosion was completed in 1965 with the creation of the Greater London Council and the division into large boroughs such as Enfield, Barnet and Hillingdon. Thus, the former homeland of the Middle Saxons, which stretched from Staines and Uxbridge in the west to Edmonton and Tottenham in the east, passed into official limbo; although the name survives to this day in postal addresses and the well known Middlesex County Cricket Club.

The tramway era represents a brief, but important, interlude in the history of the county. In 1861, George Francis Train, an American with an eye to improve the public transport system, was the instigator of two short horse tramways – one along Victoria Street and the other in Bayswater Road. Both lines were experimental and both failed to impress the local carriage folk of Middlesex, who effectively had the power to have the rails removed after only a few months of operation. Those with power and influence deemed the whole set up a public nuisance; Mr Train and all his works were sent packing.

This false start contributed to the prejudice against tramways in Westminster and the West End. The idea was openly expressed that those who could not afford to patronise an omnibus must expect to use Shanks's Pony to get to work!

In spite of these setbacks, a clutch of schemes was put forward by tramway promoters. Investors were invited to subscribe to enterprises that wished to lay rails in the highways and byways of the county. Two of the more fanciful proposals envisaged horse trams plying from Watford to Hyde Park, and serving the Great North Road well beyond the urban area.

The engineering drawing illustrates clearly that the first horse trams in North London were substantially constructed from the best materials. The solid design and dead weight of the vehicle limited the speed and added to the travails of the pulling horses. The upper deck seating layout, as on similarly configured horse buses, was referred to as 'knifeboard'.

An official brake to entrepreneurs was applied by the Tramways Act of 1870, which gave local authorities the right to veto the laying of tracks. The effects of this legislation endured for decades, long after horse power had given way to electric traction. Vital connections and extensions to the metropolitan tramway system failed to materialise because of the restrictive provisions of the Act.

Members of the upper echelons of society also noted that others who had much to benefit from the Tramways Act were artisans and labourers. The fact that workmen's fares were cheap and would aid the mobility of working people was seen as further evidence that tramcars should be excluded from well-to-do areas.

In such an atmosphere it is perhaps surprising that street tramways got going at all, but the more pragmatic and enlightened local authorities quickly realised that companies promoting the new form of transport were under an obligation to maintain the roadway adjacent to the tracks, and, furthermore, unlike omnibus proprietors, they had to pay an annual rent into council coffers.

Construction of the first lines began in 1869 and the section between Whitechapel and Bow Bridge was inaugurated for passenger traffic on 9th May 1870. The recently constituted North Metropolitan Tramways Company provided five cars for the service, which ran at ten minute intervals. Interestingly, the competing London General Omnibus Company was contracted to supply the horses. Over the next two decades the system expanded, so that by 1891 trams could be seen on most of the main roads leading from Middlesex to the gates of the City of London. Another enterprise, the London Street Tramways Company, had opened for business on 27th November 1871, when horsecars started to traverse the Hampstead Road, north of Euston Road. Eventually, trams would reach their outer termini at Hampstead, Parliament Hill, Archway Tavern and Holloway. At the latter two locations connection was made with the North Metropolitan Company.

The third company in our area of study was in many respects one of the most innovative. The North London Suburban Tramways Company was registered in December 1878 and received its Act of Parliament in the following year. Appropriately, construction started at Tramway Avenue, Edmonton, where the depot was situated. Horse trams opened for service on 10th April 1881. After building a line from Ponders End to Stamford Hill the original company failed financially and was reconstituted, this time without the word 'suburban' in the title.

Knifeboard seating on the 'outside' also features on this attractive card produced for the Raphael Tuck Company. Tuck's greeting and artistic cards first appeared in 1866, and it made sense for this London based firm to include an impression of a North Metropolitan horsecar – a vehicle with which many would have been familiar. Note the conductor in his uniform and the wooden lattice shutters, which added an element of privacy for lower deck passengers.

The new regime lived up to its name in constructing routes from Seven Sisters Corner to Finsbury Park, and from Manor House to Wood Green Town Hall. A more substantial rail section was used in anticipation of the introduction of steam tram engines. This latest form of tramway traction was inaugurated between Ponders End and Stamford Hill on 1st April 1885. In a world attuned to the leisurely pace of horse drawn traffic, the steam tram engines hauling their double deck, open top passenger trailers made an instant impact. Arguably, they provided the first regular and mechanically reliable powered transport on the highways of the capital. Contemporary observers noted that, after the novelty had worn off, loaded farm carts on their way from the market gardens of Enfield to Covent Garden, would pull aside from the tram track to let the steam tram past. The sound of the engine would alert the horses and they, being intelligent beasts well versed in the ways of metropolitan traffic, would automatically avoid the approaching machine. Often, all this would happen while the carter, who had risen in the early hours, caught up on lost sleep!

Travellers on the top deck of the tramcar, directly downwind from the engine, ran the risk of being covered in smuts as the machine exerted itself to pull a heavy load away from stops. It is also worth recording that not only passengers were transported. The two capacious platforms of each vehicle were often loaded with an assortment of items such as large flower baskets, workmen's tool boxes, parcels and packages, plus the odd bundle of washing!

The steam trams revolutionised public transport. All the local worthies seem to want to get in on the action, as this locomotive and trailer pause for the photographer. It is safe to assume that the engine driver was not obliged to turn out in top hat and tails for his normal service runs. The well attired gentlemen were probably directors and officials of the tramway company. Inspecting your investment was a very formal affair in those days! For the technically minded, the steam tram engine was built by Merryweather & Sons and had a wheelbase of 5 feet (1524mm); the double deck trailer was constructed by the Falcon Car Works.

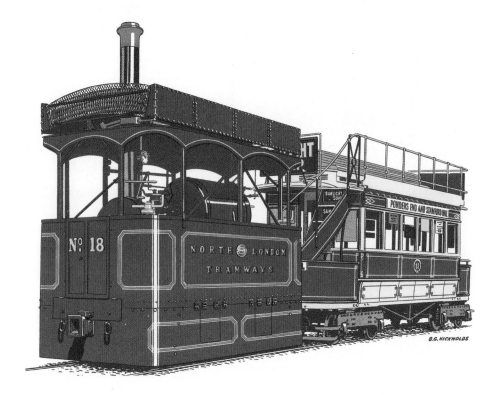

However, in spite of their usefulness, the financial storm clouds were soon gathering over the North London Company's trams. Trackbase and rails deteriorated under the pounding of the heavy steam engines. Complaints from the public about smoke emission and noise, coupled with increasingly frequent derailments that caused interruptions to the service, brought matters to a head. The much vaunted reliability of the steam trams was now in tatters.

In June 1890 the company went into liquidation and this triggered an intensive round of negotiations, the outcome of which was the acceptance by the county council of an offer by the North Metropolitan Tramways Company to take over the moribund North London operation. Steam trams rather than horsecars were put out to pasture. Equine traction was resumed on 1st August 1891. The driver of the first horsecar that day was L.J. Hobbs. He later recalled in a letter to the *TOT Staff Magazine* for October 1926 that he could remember the cornfields next to the main road by the depot in Tramway Avenue.

Thus, Middlesex County Council (MCC) had thrown its hat into the tramway ring, albeit in the role of an honest broker to restore public transport to the area. The seed had been planted for the future public/private co-operation which saw the birth of the Metropolitan Electric Tramways system.

The final piece in the jigsaw of the MET's antecedents belongs to the horse tramway that served the Harrow Road from Harlesden to Lock Bridge, Paddington. Opened on 7th July 1888, the cars traversed a natural traffic route along one of the main arteries into London. Less favoured, in terms of passengers, was the company's short branch line along Chippenham Road and Cambridge Road in the direction of Kilburn. Unfortunately for the company, which had initially set out as a purely

Middlesex based operation, local government and boundary changes absorbed part of both lines into the area of the London County Council and later into the Metropolitan Boroughs of Kensington and Paddington. Consequently, official objections and bureaucratic red tape effectively torpedoed the company's expansion plans to Stonebridge Park and Kilburn High Road. The Chippenham Road branch became a white elephant; it bears the dubious distinction of being one of the first tramway abandonments in the capital, having had an intermittent working life of barely six years. Rather perversely, the statutory rights of the company over the rusting rails were kept alive by operating a single 'ghost tram' once every three months. This practice continued at least until the autumn of 1907.

Horse tramways also existed from Shepherd's Bush to Acton, and from Hammersmith to Kew Bridge. Parts of this system, operated by West Metropolitan Tramways, dated back to 1874. This outfit was eventually acquired by the London United Tramways, a company incorporated on 19th July 1894. The LUT was to become an important tramway presence in Middlesex and in the adjoining county of Surrey; however, its sphere of influence was limited. In an agreement signed with the MCC on 28th November 1901, the London United voluntarily relinquished any interest in promoting lines north of its main Uxbridge Road route. This accord between the MCC and the LUT meant that the MET remained the major player elsewhere in the county.

As the nineteenth century drew to a close, horse trams became lighter and were equipped with transverse 'garden' seats on the top deck. The crew of this North Metropolitan car are about to set off from Edmonton in the direction of Manor House and Finsbury Park, following the route of the defunct steam trams. *LCC Tramways Trust Collection*

A lone horsecar is depicted at Cambridge Heath, Cambridge Road on the through service from Tottenham to Aldgate. Unfortunately, this useful facility would be axed when electric traction was introduced. Changing cars at the county boundary was a retrograde step imposed when the North Metropolitan lines were divided up between the MET and the London County Council.

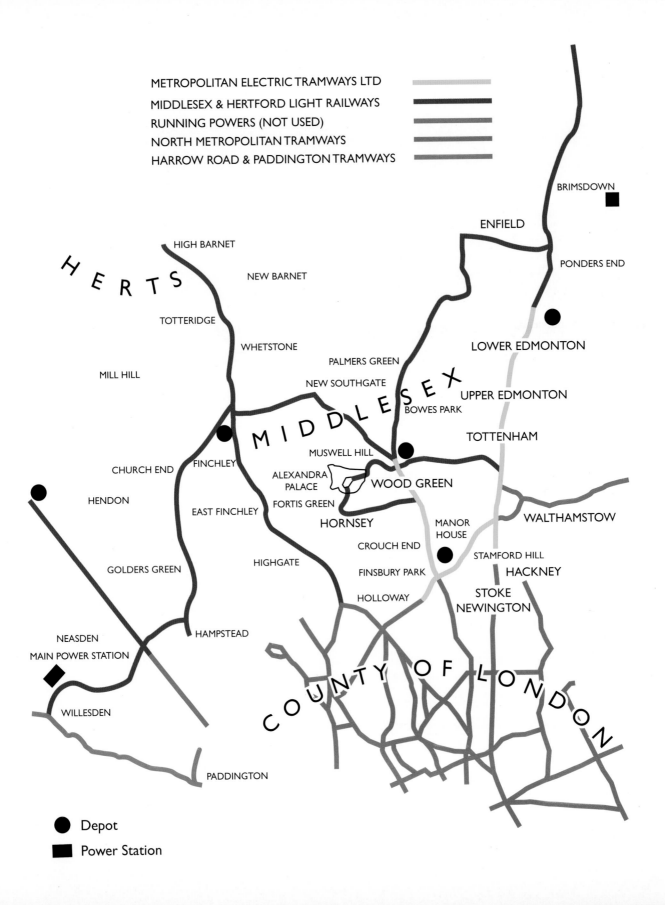

METROPOLITAN ELECTRIC TRAMWAYS LTD
MIDDLESEX & HERTFORD LIGHT RAILWAYS
RUNNING POWERS (NOT USED)
NORTH METROPOLITAN TRAMWAYS
HARROW ROAD & PADDINGTON TRAMWAYS

HERTS

MIDDLESEX

COUNTY OF LONDON

HIGH BARNET
NEW BARNET
TOTTERIDGE
WHETSTONE
MILL HILL
PALMERS GREEN
NEW SOUTHGATE
BOWES PARK
CHURCH END
FINCHLEY
MUSWELL HILL
ALEXANDRA PALACE
WOOD GREEN
FORTIS GREEN
HENDON
EAST FINCHLEY
HORNSEY
MANOR HOUSE
WALTHAMSTOW
CROUCH END
GOLDERS GREEN
HIGHGATE
FINSBURY PARK
STAMFORD HILL
HACKNEY
HOLLOWAY
STOKE NEWINGTON
HAMPSTEAD
NEASDEN
MAIN POWER STATION
WILLESDEN
PADDINGTON

BRIMSDOWN
ENFIELD
PONDERS END
LOWER EDMONTON
UPPER EDMONTON
TOTTENHAM

● Depot

■ Power Station

2. ELECTRIC TRACTION

Only in the 1890s did electric traction become a viable and commercially attractive method of powering street tramways. Across the Atlantic in the United States rapid developments in technology and vehicle design provided operators in urban areas with reliable mass transit networks. Fares were cheap and services frequent. Trams could tackle gradients and hills with ease; along the new routes suburban housing catered for the increasing numbers who wished to ride to work in the city. Although this pattern of growth was also repeated throughout Britain, London was slow off the mark. Opponents pointed out that the centre of the capital was already well served with buses. If one wanted to travel further out, they opined, then the underground and suburban railways would suffice. Aesthetes wrote letters to the press expressing their horror at the prospect of 'so many noble vistas' being 'disfigured' by ugly over-head wires. And thus the debate rumbled on.

More practical concerns exercised the minds of the inhabitants of Leeds and South Staffordshire, as they welcomed their new electric trams in November 1891 and January 1893 respectively. High on their list of priorities was a reliable way of getting to and from work. The other members of the household could also benefit. The phrase 'Let's go shopping by tram' entered the language.

Of course, there were other competing systems such as cable tramways and battery power. A contemporary report suggests that a yellow painted battery tram was tried out in Tottenham during 1891, but in spite of these novel approaches to traction, the overhead wire trolley system seemed to outperform its rivals. In the Home Counties, the people of the ancient Cinque Port of Dover celebrated on 6th September 1897. Here the trams were owned by the town council and not by private enterprise. This prospect of running a lucrative municipal transport system soon drew visitors to Dover from towns and cities across the land. Council delegations were also tempted overseas to inspect successful electric tramway installations on the Continent of Europe. The stage was set for the widespread implementation of electric traction in the UK.

Ironically, just as reports of the new transport wonder of the age were reaching the council chambers of Middlesex, London and Hertfordshire, most of the elected representatives seemed to be totally unaware of what was happening on their own doorstep. On 13th May 1898, four small single deck cars began operation on a short stretch of electric tramway linking the eastern gates of Alexandra Park with Alexandra Palace. The line was standard gauge (4ft 8½ins/1435mm) double track and was laid on private ground. Each tramcar could accommodate fifty seated and fourteen standing passengers.

One of the attractions for visitors arriving by tram was a menagerie, where accommodation for the inmates must have been at a premium. In order to alleviate the situation, eight bears were temporarily housed in the mess hut used by the tram drivers. No one in authority seems to have thought to mention this to the unfortunate motormen before they came on duty and the consequences of this oversight were quite predictable. Driver J.F. Vernon, who recounted his experiences many years later to the London Transport staff news magazine *Pennyfare*, may have had only a passing acquaintance with William Shakespeare's *The Winter's Tale*, but he surely must have heeded the famous stage direction – 'Exit. Pursued by a Bear'! Fortunately this contretemps did not dent Mr Vernon's enthusiasm and he went on to have a successful career as a driver on the Central Line.

The Alexandra Palace Electric Railway, as the tramway was known, was fated to have an ephemeral existence. Just over a fortnight after opening, an accident caused by skidding on wet rails effectively ruled out future operation in inclement weather. This decision obviously had its effect on the finances and, although the line kept its head above water for the rest of the year, the following 1899 season was a disaster. When the Palace and its associated attractions closed for the winter on 30th September, operation of the tramway ceased for good. A home was found for the fleet at Grimsby, where, after some extensive rebuilding, the cars ran until 1925.

This little line deserves to be remembered by Londoners. Many historians consider 4th April 1901 as the date when the capital's first electric tramway opened. In fact the LUT services in West London were inaugurated almost three years after the launch of the Alexandra Palace line.

After this romantic interlude of a palace with escaping bears, the history of the promotion of the MET may sound rather staid and humdrum. However, there were enough twists and turns in the plot to keep the locals interested. The principal players were, on one side, the members of the MCC's Light Railways & Tramways Committee, and on the other, the representatives of the privately owned British Electric Traction Company. This latter organisation had acquired a controlling interest in the Metropolitan Tramways and Omnibus Company, which had previously been unsuccessful in promoting tramways in the Middlesex area. The BET holds an important place in the promotion and construction of tramways in the UK. It filled the gap, where local authorities were unable or unwilling to run their own tramcars. The BET was also implacably opposed to what was then termed 'municipal trading' and it took the fight to council chambers and to Parliament in order to champion private enterprise.

It is also important to note that the County Council had a change of heart in 1899 and the members resolved to use new legislation as set out in the Light Railways Act of 1896, rather than the more cumbersome, expensive and time consuming Tramways Act of 1870. Thus, the MCC's electric tramways were always classified officially as Light Railways. Matters concerning street tramways at this time were supervised on a governmental level by the Board of Trade, which fulfilled much the same function as the modern day Department of Transport. A fully fledged Ministry of Transport was not created until 1919. Since it was apparent that the BET and MCC had positioned themselves on different sides of the tramway divide, it probably came as a surprise to the BET's shareholders that the company they owned was in talks with the opposition. However, the *BET Monthly Gazette* was already in optimistic mood, when it reported in September 1900:

The (MET) Company have promoted about 23 miles of Light Railways in the North of London which have been recommended by the Light Railway Commissioners, four miles having already received the approval of the Board of Trade.

The discussions between the two parties can be characterised as taking place in an atmosphere of pragmatic horse trading, with the result that, on 16th November 1900, a public/private deal was struck. The main provisions of the agreement can be summarised as follows:

The MET as constituted by its British Electric Traction parent company would supply the rolling stock to a design agreeable to the County Council. The operating company would also maintain the permanent way and the tramcars to an acceptable standard, as determined by inspecting officers of the Council. The MCC would finance and supervise the construction of the tram track and would attend to the reconstruction and widening of bridges and roads. The Council would also furnish land suitable for depots and generating stations. Depot buildings, underground cables, generating and overhead equipment were to come within the ambit of the Company. The MET would also be responsible for the payment of an annual rent to the Council, the final amount being determined partly on a fixed and partly on a profit sharing basis. The Company's lease was extended to 31st December 1930.

This contract proved a sound basis to begin the process of constructing and operating the tram system. A similar working arrangement was later concluded with representatives of Hertfordshire County Council, in whose domain lay the outer termini of Barnet and Waltham Cross.

After the deal had been brokered, there then came a flurry of activity, as applications were posted for Light Railway Orders and the MET obtained possession of the remaining sections of horse tramway situated north of the LCC boundary.

In November 1902 the *BET Monthly Gazette* commented:

The purchase price to be paid by the Company to the North Metropolitan Tramways Company for the eight miles of tramway in Middlesex has been agreed, and includes two leasehold depots, 62 cars and 600 horses &c. As soon as the Board of Trade sanction the transfer, these tramways will be taken over and worked by the Company by horse traction, until they are reconstructed for electric traction.

The takeover occurred on 26th November 1902 and it was noted that the first MET employees numbered some 333 men, of whom 216 were drivers and conductors. Further good news followed, as the MET acquired a majority shareholding in the Harrow Road and Paddington Tramways Company. It is important to remember that, although the MET system was conceived as a unified network, the former North Metropolitan horsecar lines plus the Harrow Road route were owned directly by the Company and were never part of the Middlesex County Council's light railways scheme.

The year 1902 ended with the MCC having secured sites for sub-stations in Wood Green and Finchley. The Council also agreed contracts for the permanent way and associated highway alterations on three sections of the new system: Edgware to Cricklewood, Highgate Archway to Whetstone and Wood Green to Tottenham. These were considered as precursors to a large system, but as we shall see, this grandiose vision of the county being criss-crossed by a network of tramlines was soon brought down to earth by financial constraints and uncooperative local authorities, some of whom were only too happy to demand that expensive road paving and street lighting schemes should be charged to the tramways account.

The handful of passengers on car 31 is almost outnumbered by BET company officials. It was important in these very early stages of electric tramway operation to keep a watchful eye open for any potential delays or mechanical problems. The vehicle is seen at the Tottenham boundary on the first section of line to open.
D. Jones Collection

The first tramway on the list – the Edgware to Cricklewood route – is a classic example of how ancient county and parish boundaries could affect tramway development. Mere lines on a map, as these divisions may have appeared, could not hinder the journey to work for most bus and train passengers in the capital. However, when a tramway was projected into a neighbouring area outside Middlesex, then organised groups of objectors and local councils with an anti-tram bias could delay or totally scotch the best laid plans of the MCC. In short, without the support of the local authority no rails could be laid, and as we shall see in the next chapter, not even the findings of a Royal Commission could get this vital route constructed. Thus it was, that the pious hope of a trunk route from the West End of London right out as far as Watford remained a pipe dream.

As regards the northern extension from Edgware, the active support of Hertfordshire County Council was regarded, at first, as a promising sign of future success, but delaying tactics from protestors, inter council wrangles and financial worries put paid to the scheme. South of The Crown, Cricklewood, the prospects looked even bleaker. This was LCC territory and the elected representatives at London's County Hall were obliged to listen to any objections put forward by individual Metropolitan Boroughs. Opposition from the Hampstead and St Marylebone councils effectively killed off any tramway presence on their respective territories. No MET tramcar would ever reach Kilburn or Maida Vale!

Another county boundary, this time in the shadow of Highgate's famous Archway, was set to be the starting point for the new tracks to Finchley and Whetstone. Here the outlook was more positive than that at Cricklewood. The LCC had plans to electrify the horse tramway that terminated at Archway Tavern and, therefore, it obviously made sense for the two systems to meet.

Attention now turned to the 8.3 miles (13.3 km) of former North Metropolitan horse tramway that was owned outright by the MET. Messrs Dick, Kerr & Co. Ltd were awarded the contract for the reconstruction of lines from Finsbury Park to Manor House and Wood Green, from Manor House to Edmonton and from Seven Sisters Corner to Stamford Hill.

In January 1904 the *BET Monthly Gazette* reported:

Over two-thirds of the eight and a half miles of tramways have been reconstructed by the contractors, and nearly all the low-tension cables have been laid. The erection of overhead equipment has commenced. Two of the old depots are in course of adaptation for the housing of electric cars.

The contractors to the Middlesex County Council have completed three-fourths of the permanent way of eleven and half miles of Light Railways which form the first section, and the Company's contractors are progressing satisfactorily with the cable laying. Sites for car sheds and sub-stations have been obtained at Hendon and Finchley, and contracts for the building will be let at an early date. It is expected that the North Metropolitan Electric Power Supply Company, from whom the electrical energy required for working the system is to be purchased, will be able to give a supply of current for experimental purposes in March or April.

The two old depots mentioned above refer to ex-horsecar sheds at Wood Green by Jolly Butchers Hill, and at Edmonton by Tramway Avenue. A large power station to cater for the new electric tramways was built by the River Lee (also known as the River Lea) at Brimsdown. The owning company, later known as Northmet Power, was part of the BET group. The Northmet subsequently purchased the Willesden Urban District Council's power station in Harlesden, and this building would eventually supply current for the MET's western lines.

The intention, as expressed in the article, that experimental running of trams could begin in the spring of 1904, was not to be fulfilled. Some 70 vehicles had been ordered from the Brush Electrical Engineering Company. Delivery of the first 35 cars from the works at Loughborough to Wood Green Depot probably commenced at the end of April. The last car of the second half of the batch finally turned up at Edmonton Depot in August.

All the new trackwork and overhead was now nearing completion. The only fly in the ointment was an objection from the LCC to the line from Manor House to Finsbury Park, but matters were ironed out by May, so that the official inspection by the Board of Trade could take place on 19th July 1904. Major J.W. Pringle RE of the Board of Trade was duly diligent in his task. He was accompanied by Mr A.P. Trotter, who checked all the electric equipment along the route. Both gentlemen were satisfied with the soundness of the enterprise and a Certificate of Fitness was issued, with the proviso that the maximum speed of the tramcars be set at 10mph (16km/h).

Car 31 makes a repeat appearance on the Seven Sisters Road opposite the entrance to Wilberforce Road. The track along which the tram is travelling is situated in the County of Middlesex, whilst the adjacent tramlines, leading to Finsbury Park, lie in London County Council territory.
D. Jones Collection

The great day dawned on Friday, 22nd July 1904. The inauguration involved top officials and directors of the MET and BET, together with representatives of the press, one of whose members penned the following description for the *Tramway & Railway World*:

. . . The party travelled by special train from Liverpool Street Station to Brimsdown, Enfield, where they went over the power station. Subsequently they drove to the Edmonton car depot, where a sub-station is being erected, and continued the journey by way of Lordship Lane to the Wood Green depot, where a sub-station is now in working order. There electric cars were in waiting and in these the party traversed the lines now open. The route was from Wood Green through Green Lanes to Finsbury Park, and along Seven Sisters Road to Tottenham High Road. The party returned to the city by brakes.

The article went on to detail technical aspects of the Metropolitan Electric Tramways; the lines concerned were, of course, wholly owned by the MET, and it must have given the BET some quiet satisfaction to steal a march on their MCC partners! The first County Council route should have opened at the same time, but it had been delayed by construction difficulties.

The celebrations attracted a fair crowd of Londoners, eager to witness at first hand one of the new mechanical marvels of the age. Unfortunately, just about all of the spectators present would not have had the wherewithal to hire a carriage to return to the city. Many had to rely on the slow and outdated horse trams, which now looked totally antiquated compared to the sleek electric models across the county boundary at Finsbury Park. Anecdotal evidence suggests that a small section of the crowd on the London County Council side of the road began to jeer the arrival of each horse tram at the terminus. Sentiments expressed were along the lines that 'Dobbin should be put out to grass' and that the LCC 'should pull its socks up' in getting its side of this main route electrified – the ratepayers were becoming unsettled! Of course, all this was music to the ears of the BET, who could point out that this was

The Middlesex County Council lines opened with some style. School children were given time off to witness the inauguration of electric traction. Everyone seems to have turned out smartly for 'special car' 100. Wearing a hat in those days was absolutely *de rigueur*!
D. Jones Collection

one more example of municipal trading falling down on the job. However, the house magazine, the *BET Monthly Gazette*, although at times critical of the shortcomings of just about every other publicly owned tramway in the land, maintained a proper diplomatic stance towards Middlesex.

The Middlesex County Council's light railways finally got the green light at an official opening of the Wood Green to Bruce Grove route on 20th August 1904. This time the BET took a back seat, as the County Council, with the great and the good in attendance, organised in sumptuous style a splendid event at Bruce Castle. Accounts published later would suggest that the pomp and circumstance of the day cost about eight times more than the BET spent on their inauguration of the Finsbury Park line. Indeed, this was municipal trading on a grand scale!

Flags and bunting were out on Bruce Grove and Lordship Lane, as a procession of six decorated tramcars travelled from Tottenham to Wood Green. The formal opening was conducted by Sir Francis Cory-Wright, Chairman of the Light Railways and Tramways Committee of the Middlesex County Council. The leading vehicle was car 71, suitably emblazoned with the legend COUNTY COUNCIL OF MIDDLESEX, picked out on the waist panel in gold letters on a vermilion (bright signal red) background. The lower or rocker panel of the tram was painted ivory and bore the lettering METROPOLITAN ELECTRIC TRAMWAYS LTD in black.

After reaching Wood Green, the convoy turned south to Finsbury Park, where the cars reversed to head out over Seven Sisters Road to the eastern end of Bruce Grove, Tottenham. Unfortunately, a low bridge at Bruce Grove (GER) Station prevented the completion of a circular trip. The remedial work to fill this short gap would involve lowering the road under the bridge. The through service was eventually opened for traffic on 11th April 1906.

It was reported in the *BET Monthly Gazette* about the events of the twentieth that . . . *although the first public car only commenced running at five in the evening, the number of passengers carried on this route exceeded 12,000, and the earnings for the evening amounted to 34d per car-mile.*

Adjustments had to be made to the roadway and the railway bridge at Bruce Grove before the Lordship Lane service could be extended to join new tracks in Hertford Road. Brand new car 93 seems to be surrounded by the local newspaper boys, one of whom appears to have the motorman's point iron in his possession. The two ladies on the top deck probably thought they were being very daring.
D. Jones Collection

Meanwhile on the previous day, when all eyes were fixed on the forthcoming gala event at Bruce Castle, the Board of Trade inspector had passed fit for service the new MET line from Brantwood Road, near the Edmonton/Tottenham boundary to Stamford Hill via Seven Sisters Corner. Cars started working the extended route from Finsbury Park to Brantwood Road on 24th August 1904 – on this occasion accompanied by little or no official celebrations. The section south from Seven Sisters Corner to Stamford Hill was not opened at this time. BET sources suggest that the Company was waiting to complete the connection in Bruce Grove, so that electric trams could run from Wood Green to Stamford Hill. Therefore, horsecars maintained the service; as they continued to do on the route north of Brantwood Road to Tramway Avenue, Edmonton. At the end of October 1904 a short extension from Brantwood Road to the southern end of Fore Street, Edmonton provided a much needed stabling siding for cars reversing to await football crowds from the nearby Tottenham Hotspurs ground at White Hart Lane.

Attention now turned to the first of the western routes to be completed in the 1904 inaugural phase of the MET. In strict legal terms, these were light railways not tramways, but this fine distinction probably meant nothing to the average passenger. The Edgware to Cricklewood Boundary line opened on 3rd December. Again, there were no reported celebrations. Perhaps by now the accountants had put a damper on unnecessary expenditure. The novelty may also have worn off with the public, because the number of passengers carried on the fifteen cars allocated to the new Hendon Depot was disappointingly low. However, the route was still isolated from the rest of the system and the Edgware Road, north of Hendon, was still mostly open country, with little traffic to be carried on the trams.

End of year figures quoted in the (renamed) *BET Gazette* give the number of horsecars as 8, with 107 electric vehicles. Of the 411 employees listed, no fewer than 249 were drivers and conductors. A grand total of 15.13 route miles (24.35 km) was open for traffic. All seemed set fair for a successful future; however, a note of caution was sounded in an issue of *The Home Counties Magazine* for 1904.

This was an era when the Express Boot Co., Cricklewood, could sole and heel your footwear in 20 minutes. You could save some shoe leather by travelling on board car 95. It loads passengers at the county boundary in Cricklewood Broadway, opposite Ash Grove. This 'terminus' was forced on the MET by parochial squabbles and served no real commercial purpose after competing bus services could traverse the Edgware Road to reach the real traffic objectives of the West End and central London.

This fine view of one of the initial batch of BET tramcars shows that these vehicles were built to exacting specifications. Note especially the cream painted, wrought iron tracery around the top deck and the wire mesh 'dog guard' between the trucks. As its name suggests, this was placed to prevent inquisitive cats or canines getting trapped underneath the car.
D. Jones Collection

The editor had obviously been sent an MET prospectus, which caused him to reflect on the expansion plans of the tramway company. The notion of rails stretching as far as Watford, Cheshunt and Woodford filled him with a sense of unease. His remark: 'We all know that the coming of the tram means the going of the country' was echoed by many campaigners, who wished to preserve rural England. This statement was followed by a very prescient observation: 'Much less to be dreaded – indeed it is to be welcomed – is the establishment of regular motor (bus) services, along suitable roads, from railway stations to outlying villages'.

When electric trams first arrived in High Road, Wood Green, the road surface had to be improved to a certain standard. The operating company was only liable for that portion of the highway nearest the outer rails and between the tracks. From the look of it, there still seems to be some work to be done. On this warm summer's day of a century ago, the local authority watering cart needs to make an appearance in order to clean up and lay the dust.
D. Jones Collection

Highgate Archway, London

43166

3. GREAT NORTH ROAD

After the Middlesex County Council witnessed at first hand the benefits of electric traction, there could be no doubt as to the usefulness of the new form of transport. Following on from the initial success of the events in 1904, the pace of construction increased. In the period from January 1905 to February 1911, when the system was completed, there were no fewer than thirty-three inaugurations of new sections of track. The planning and implementation of new routes was based on the logic of supplying quality public transport to the main trunk roads leading from the centre of London. Arguably, the first major traffic artery of the MET was the Great North Road, described in this chapter together with the western routes. The other was the Hertford Road and the associated tramways on the eastern side of the county. Connecting lines joined these spokes of the wheel, so that there was eventually a continuous radial tramline from Acton to Tottenham via Harlesden, Cricklewood, North Finchley, Wood Green and Bruce Grove. The only sections that patently did not fit this pattern were the two routes serving Alexandra Palace and the service along Southbury Road, Enfield.

In view of the potential competition from suburban railways, motor buses and projected tube lines, it was also a strategic necessity for the MET to establish some form of through running with the London County Council trams. With such an arrangement in place, the financial viability of the system would be secured, because services would be relevant to the needs of the local population, including commuters to central London.

In order to see how the MET fitted in with the rest of its competitors, it is worth digressing to consider one of the major transport events of 1905 – the convening of the Royal Commission on London Traffic.

The proceedings of the Commission in respect of plans and proposed solutions for the County of London are described in detail in the author's *LCC Electric Tramways*. In terms of the effect on the expanding MET, one of the main witnesses called to give evidence was J.L. Devonshire, Managing Director of the MET since July 1902. He obviously saw the disadvantage of promoting any metropolitan electric tramway network that would be forced by restrictive legislation and local vetoes into a series of isolated routes with dead end termini well short of the real traffic objectives. He also advocated a common management strategy that would eventually lead to a unified system of lines, which served the best interests of Londoners.

The Royal Commission was broadly in favour of street tramways and it made a number of recommendations in the form of 23 proposed new routes. Those of direct relevance to the MET are quoted from the published report of the Commission:

The tram service has now been extended down the hill to terminate by Archway Tavern. Car 77 is depicted on the north side of Highgate Archway after the Bank Holiday crowds have disappeared.
D. Jones Collection

Route 6. Edgware Road and Maida Vale – A surface tramway starting near the Marble Arch and passing along Edgware Road, Maida Vale and High Road, Kilburn, and terminating by a junction with the existing light railways of the Middlesex County Council at Cricklewood.

Route 7. Harrow Road – A surface tramway, starting by a junction with the Harrow Road and Paddington Tramways at their eastern terminus in Harrow Road, and passing along Harrow Road, Westbourne Terrace and Bishops Road, and terminating by a junction with Routes 6 and 22 in the Edgware Road.

Route 8. Cambridge Avenue – A surface tramway, starting by a junction with the Harrow Road and Paddington Tramways at their terminus in Cambridge Road, and passing along Cambridge Avenue and terminating by a junction with Route 6 in Edgware Road.

Route 22. Marylebone and Euston Roads – A surface tramway, starting by a junction with Route 7 at the Edgware Road opposite the Harrow Road, and passing along the suggested new street and the Marylebone Road and Euston Road, and terminating by a junction with the LCC tramways in the Euston Road, at Kings Cross Station.

Route 23. Finchley Road – A surface tramway, starting by a junction with Route 22 at Upper Baker Street, and passing along Upper Baker Street, Park Road, Wellington Road and Finchley Road, and terminating by a junction with Middlesex County Council authorised light railways at Childs Hill.

The result of all this was very disappointing. In fact, only the Harrow Road section was later constructed, and then with a slight deviation from the Commission's recommended route. The references to surface tramways were intended to make the distinction between street based and sub-surface lines, as demonstrated by the LCC's Kingsway Tram Subway.

Publication of the final report did have the effect of galvanising the opposition, such as Sir George Bartley, an implacable foe of any tramway promoter who wished to foist tramcars on central London and on the unwilling City gents of the Square Mile. He was of the opinion that:

The Report seems to suggest that motor omnibuses will not take the place of tramways . . . the evidence does not appear to be conclusive either way, though tending rather in favour of motor omnibuses than the reverse.

Thus, the prospect of the electric tram becoming, as it did in almost all of the world's capital cities, the prime form of public transport, evaporated in the face of sustained opposition. A worrying picture is painted by the official statistics for London's bus companies. In 1905 there were 241 motor buses, but by 1912 – one year after the opening of last MET extension – the internal combustion engine was well and truly in the ascendant with 2,908 registered motor buses.

It can be argued that the elected members of Middlesex County Council should have been more aware of the advances being made in motor bus technology. Whilst it is true that some of the ardour towards the County Council's light railways had cooled somewhat by the end of the first decade of the twentieth century, it is also quite evident that the supporters of tramways could point to many positive benefits.

The average electric tram was mechanically reliable and could transport a larger load than a single motor bus. Tramways were considered an important factor in the establishment of large scale local authority housing projects, such as the LCC development in Tottenham at the White Hart Lane Estate. The MET line in Lordship Lane would eventually form the southern boundary of the planned new housing. Many of the recently enfranchised electors relied on cheap fares, which could not be matched by the buses. In the *BET Gazette* for March 1907 it was claimed that a one penny (0.41p) fare on a MET tram could take a workman or artisan a maximum distance of five and half miles (8.8 km)!

Although the Advisory Board of Engineers to the Royal Commission had considered a proper width for thoroughfares carrying tramways as an ideal 48 feet (14.6 metres) between kerbs, roads traversed by the MET tramcars were typically some ten to twelve feet (3 – 3.6 metres) broader than the Commission's suggestion. Thus each reconstructed highway, financed by the tramways, benefited all road users, not just the tramcars. The irony of this lies in the fact that a good road surface was just what competing buses needed.

The other highlight of 1905 was undoubtedly one of which most of the members of the Commission could approve – the inauguration, on 7th June, of the main line from Highgate Archway to Whetstone. A trial run, carrying some of the MET's engineering staff, took place on 19th May. The vehicle used was car 125, which belonged to Type A. The Company had decided to group its fleet into different *types* rather than *classes* as employed by the LCC. This minor distinction, ignorance of which has tripped up many transport historians unaware of some of the more arcane ways of London tramways, was perpetuated well into London Transport days.

The opening ceremony of the Great North Road route is imminent. No doubt all concerned are anxious that the big day goes off well. Unfortunately, this grand occasion seems to have caught the highway contractors unprepared. An untidy heap of woodblock setts obstructs the road next to car 123.
D. Jones Collection

25

The original terminus was in the shadow of the famous Highgate Archway. As depicted here, trams are arriving and departing fully loaded. A couple of policemen, standing in the roadway behind car 117, are on hand to regulate the crowds and to stop a free-for-all. The 'queuing principle', so beloved by the inhabitants of our islands, was not entrenched in British culture until the time of the First World War. *D. Jones Collection*

The impact of the new trunk service on the historic Great North Road cannot be ignored. Even the pomp and circumstance of the previous year's opening ceremonies returned in part for the occasion, as the splendidly named Sir Francis Cory-Wright, was again on hand to guide the first car past a cheering throng of onlookers. No stops were permitted until the party reached North Finchley, where a convenient break was made to inspect the new depot, situated between Woodberry Grove and Rosemount Avenue. It was then on to the terminus at Totteridge Lane, Whetstone, before a brisk non-stop return to Highgate Archway.

Straight away, a through fare of just 3d (1.2p) found a large and very appreciative clientele. The penny workman's ticket for the four and a half miles (6.4km) from Whetstone to the Archway was even more of a bargain. The effect on the competing horse buses was immediate and fatal. In modern parlance, the tram route was a victim of its own success. Demand soon outstripped supply and more cars had to be drafted into the area. Even then, on fine Sundays and bank holidays, members of the Metropolitan Police were called upon to control the large crowds at each terminus.

The *BET Gazette* could hardly contain its excitement. It reported that record receipts had been recorded on Whit Monday, when over 37,000 passengers were carried on the route. It went on to say that the MET had transported around 200,000 passengers over the bank holiday weekend. Amongst these folk were many lowly paid working people from the metropolis, who could now use the tram to get out into the fresh air and fields of the countryside. This important social benefit, almost entirely overlooked by the Royal Commission, was of course grist to the mill of the well heeled tramophobes, who forecast all manner of violent disasters, when the 'hoi polloi' finally managed to explore the rural areas of their own native land.

Such snobbery was commonplace in an era when social class was paramount. Even the tramcars themselves reflected a certain social hierarchy. The open top deck with its transverse wood seats was, especially in inclement weather, mainly a male preserve. Company Bye-Law 5 of 1st January 1905 stated: 'No person shall smoke or carry lighted pipes, cigars or cigarettes inside any carriage'. This rule added to the population on the top, whilst those seated on the inside generally consisted of women, children, the elderly and the infirm. Pet owners were forbidden to bring dogs or other animals on the cars. Also excluded from the Company's vehicles were the obvious categories: drunks, people using offensive language, unfortunates afflicted with any infectious or contagious disease and anyone carrying a weapon or a loaded firearm. The tram conductor also had to exercise discretion when allowing anybody on board whose state of dress or undress might offend other passengers or damage the linings or cushions of the carriage. Finally, the modesty of any lady game enough to travel on the outside was protected by so called decency boards, which surrounded the top deck. Without this screening it was thought that the sight of shapely ankles and glimpses of petticoats could inflame the passions of male passers-by!

Although the country was now ruled by a monarch whose love of the high life in Paris and Biarritz was the stuff of popular legend, a strong sense of Victorian morality still prevailed amongst the lesser mortals of the United Kingdom. Those transgressing the Company bye-laws could expect a fine not exceeding forty shillings (£2) for each offence. This was a small fortune to the average wage earner, but local magistrates, of whom Sir Francis Cory-Wright was one, could sometimes exercise leniency.

Inspectors were appointed to supervise discipline among conductors and motor-men and their word was law in an era when an employee could be sacked on the spot for a heinous offence such as smoking or eating on duty! Tram crews arriving at Highgate probably had little time to do any illicit smoking, or anything else for that matter, other than change ends, flip the seats over and welcome another load of passengers. Although the terminus beneath Highgate Archway had the merit of being rather picturesque, in economic terms it was some few hundred yards short of the real traffic objective. At the bottom of the hill outside Archway Tavern connections could be made with three other tramways – the Highgate Hill cable line, the former London Street Tramways Company horsecar line along Junction Road to Kentish Town and Euston Road, and the former North Metropolitan route to central London via Holloway Road. Obviously, it made more sense for passengers to transfer cars at one convenient point. Planners for both county councils were aware of this fact; the only proviso was that the arrangement would have to be reviewed, when the LCC got round to electrifying the previously mentioned sections.

The LCC authorised construction of the short line from Archway to the Archway Tavern and it was inspected by the Board of Trade on 21st December 1905. Full public service commenced on 22nd December, just in time to cater for an expected Christmas rush of new passengers. The festive season also found MET and County officials, contractors and construction workers in hectic activity, preparing for the New Year, when the route was due to be extended further from the current terminus at Totteridge Lane to a crossover on the county boundary just south of the junction with Lyonsdown Road. Again, with an eye to the excursion traffic, this line was opened on Saturday, 4th August 1906, just in time for the expected deluge of punters on the following Monday's Bank Holiday.

Elegant centre poles support the overhead wires in Great North Road, North Finchley. These were later deemed to be a traffic hazard and they were removed. In the first decade of the twentieth century many motorists seemed to have had a fatal attraction for the centre poles! The vehicle illustrated is Type C/1 car 198.
D. Jones Collection

Some weeks before the August extension, a serious accident occurred which cast a shadow over all operations on the Great North Road. On 23rd June 1906, car 115 got into difficulties whilst descending the hill from Highgate Archway to the terminus at Archway Tavern. The event made newspaper headlines around the capital. The whole misfortune was picked over in the most lurid and sensational way. One of the more dramatic accounts was printed in the *Tramway & Railway World*, just seven days after the fatal crash. The graphic details were described thus by an unnamed reporter:

North London Disaster – A double-decked bogie car of the Metropolitan Electric Tramways Company got out of control of the motorman before reaching a compulsory stop at the top of the Archway Road hill, Highgate, on Saturday afternoon last. The descent is about a quarter of a mile in length, the gradient at the summit being one in 65, and at the bottom one in 30 . . .

It was only in September last that the Archway Road terminus of the Whetstone route was opened. Constructed by the London County Council, it was leased to the Middlesex County Council, which in turn leased it to the company. The driver's efforts to restrain the car were futile; it grazed two unoccupied mourning coaches, and smashed the hearse, the impact throwing several persons off the car platform. Next a furniture van was demolished, the driver being unhurt. The motorman now jumped from the tramcar, and less than a hundred yards farther on a motor omnibus filled with a pleasure party was sent crashing into the shop of Messrs Pope, jobmasters. Two men, Mansfield and Hall, were at work in the front room of the shop. Mansfield was killed instantly, and Hall died two hours later in the Great Northern Hospital. The

*bus swung round and dashed a dozen yards away into the shop front of the Archway
Restaurant, two doors below Messrs Pope's premises. A youth was mortally injured
here. The "Vanguard" (bus) remained fixed, and the occupants, several of whom had
been badly cut, were removed. The tramcar struck and overturned a hansom cab, and
the driver was badly injured.*

 *Warned by the shouts of the police on duty at this busy junction of North London
thoroughfares, pedestrians, passing vehicles and horse tramcars made for places of
safety. The runaway crashed into a tramcar at the terminus, left the metals and ran
into a heavy electric lamp standard above a refuge in the crossing by Junction Road.
This checked the car, which turned a half circle, skidded across a dozen yards of the
granite road and stopped within three feet of the shop of Messrs Isaacs at Holloway
Road . . .*

 *The passengers were in great alarm. They came out pale and shaking, and climbed
over the wrecked platforms into the street. Twenty-one persons were injured, a number
being passengers who dropped off the car.*

In an age before satellite TV and instant world events coverage, accidents usually drew the crowds and prompted local picture postcard publishers to set up camera tripods to record the scene for posterity. Such was the case, here at the Highgate tram smash, when news of the misfortune was eagerly awaited by the populace of the capital city. Clearly, extensive repairs will be needed to the staircases and driving platforms of the two stricken tramcars. Inspecting the wreckage appears to be a purely male preoccupation. *D. Jones Collection*

The report of the official enquiry, conducted by Lieutenant Colonel H.A. Yorke,
severely censured the driver, Ernest Henry Cone (some sources give the name as
Cole), for abandoning his post. The actions of the conductor Griffith Davies were
commended in that he tried to persuade passengers not to jump off the vehicle while
it was in motion. It seems that brake failure plus locking of the wheels caused
skidding on greasy rails, and this brought about the disaster. The MET was also
criticised in not giving enough training to apprentice motormen before they were put
to work on difficult gradients.

At Easter 1907 this opening day view, taken outside Barnet Church, features car 129, as it fills with locals about to indulge in the new experience of an exhilarating ride downhill to Whetstone. One suspects many of the youngsters would have been told by their parents not to stray too far – penny fares were the order of the day.

Facing page upper Car 109 is seen on Walm Lane, Willesden. Although this part of the route has been laid with double track, Middlesex County Council had to compromise further down the road, where the narrow carriageway prevented wholesale widening. Note the detail on the metal traction standards. Electric trams pioneered fixed stopping places – in theory, buses could pick up and set down passengers anywhere.
D. Jones Collection

Facing page lower Map showing the route of the thwarted extension of tramway from Canons Park to Bushey Heath.

With the recommendations of the December 1906 official accident report ringing in their ears, the Company's engineers had to double check all braking systems before the next grand opening, which occurred on 28th March 1907. The goal of reaching the historic Hertfordshire town of Chipping Barnet (also known as High Barnet or simply as Barnet) was fulfilled. The end of the track outside the imposing Parish Church of St John the Baptist was a fitting setting for the new electric cars in their smart red and white livery. The Company and its associates could now really be said to be servicing the needs of the locals, because the Northmet already had the monopoly on domestic electricity supply throughout the district. Residents now benefited from a regular service of one tram every four minutes along the Great North Road to Highgate. Extra vehicles were run on fine summer weekends and on Barnet Fair days. The well known cattle and horse fairs took place in April, September and November, and they attracted a large number of visitors to the town.

This positive approach and feeling of well-being for the Company in the Barnet area of Hertfordshire was in complete contrast to the frustration of all the wasted effort on one extension that failed to materialise. The residents of Stanmore blocked a projected line north of Edgware to the Hertfordshire boundary at Bushey Heath, thus forcing a rethink amongst the members of the Council's Light Railways Committee. After repeated attempts to force the line through, a seemingly poor compromise was reached, at least in terms of potential passenger revenue, when the Edgware to Cricklewood section received a short extension northwards to Canons Park. This was opened 31st October 1907. A more satisfactory result awaited the MET at the southern end of the route. Work on a new line from Cricklewood Broadway along Chichele Road was in an advanced stage and, on 30th March 1906, MCC Alderman Herbert Nield was at the controls of inaugural car 90, as it travelled the short distance to the interim terminus at Willesden Green Station. Further progress towards Craven Park was held up by problems in Willesden High Road.

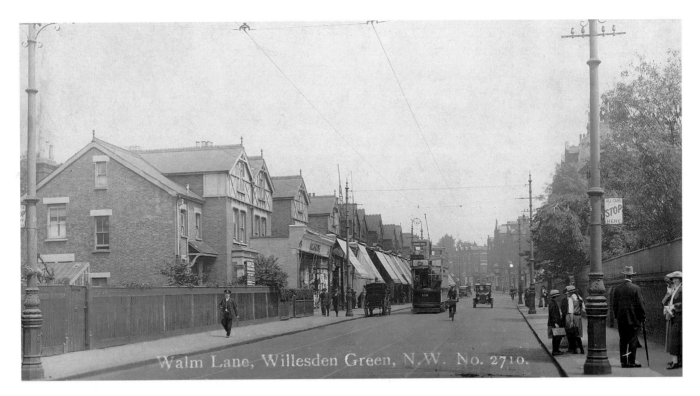

Walm Lane, Willesden Green, N.W. No. 2710.

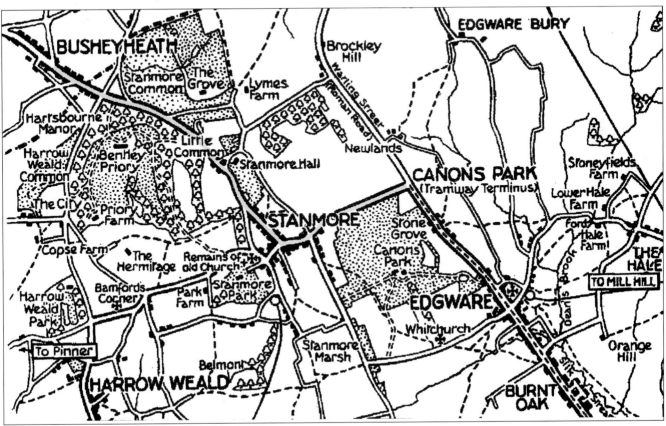

H.R.M. Series No. 70.   Electric Tram, Harlesden.

The lads on the pavement gaze in wonder as car 88 is put through its paces on a test run through Harlesden. No doubt, the trainee tram driver is prudently slowing down for the crossover outside the police station. It was not unknown for police officers with stopwatches to time trams, in order to catch speeding motormen.

It was always the intention of the MCC to have a purely double track system with no bottlenecks caused by single line working. Eventually, a compromise was reached at Willesden and two separate sections of interlaced track were installed. After all the delays and acrimony over compensation to local residents on account of road widening, it was seen as something of a diplomatic gesture by the County Council to forgo a full ceremonial opening. Service from Willesden Green Station to Craven Park began on 23rd December 1907.

At Craven Park the new Willesden line met the rails of the Harrow Road route, which had also had its fair share of construction delays. The main problem here lay with the seasonal flooding of the River Brent at Stonebridge Park. Matters were compounded by the fact that the site for the new depot was also subject to regular inundation. Negotiations with the Metropolitan Water Board about the location of new mains pipes also added to the delay. In order to get some sort of tram service on the road, a short section of route between the Iron Bridge at Stonebridge Park and the Royal Oak at Harlesden was opened for traffic on 10th October 1906. Stonebridge Park remained the end of the line until 15th April 1908, when an extension to Wembley opened. Here the County Council paused to consider its options.

Of course, the natural traffic objective of any public transport vehicle on this road was the town of Harrow. However, the combination of resistance from affluent locals and the political clout of Harrow School killed the plan. At a meeting held in Harrow

High Street, Harlesden

73689

School on 18th June 1901, Mr A.K. Carlyon, a member of the Middlesex County Council, was quoted as saying, 'The County Council has practically been forced into light railway schemes, as the London County Council had threatened to invade Middlesex with lines of the kind'. This accusation, if true, puts a different complexion on the motivation of other members of the MCC, who sanctioned the county's electric tramways. Scaremongering at the meeting in Harrow obviously paid off, with the result that a halt to the rails was called outside The Swan, Sudbury. The first fare-paying tram passengers arrived here on 24th September 1910.

At the other end of the Harrow Road, the reconstruction of the former horse tramway from Harlesden, Royal Oak to Lock Bridge over the Grand Junction Canal had also hit a few snags. At several locations road widening could not be completed, thus forcing the contractors to lay two sections of temporary single track. The full electric service to Lock Bridge opened on 22nd December 1906. This was where the trams terminated for almost the next four years. Protracted negotiations with the LCC (as described in the article overleaf), plus remedial strengthening work on the two road bridges over the canal at Lock Bridge and Warwick Crescent, delayed the extension of the line to Paddington. The official opening to passengers came on 6th December 1910. An interesting aside to all this activity was the fact that this route was one hundred percent overhead trolley operated and, as such, Paddington became the only non-conduit tram terminal in central London.

Jubilee Clock, Harlesden is a well known local landmark, and the area was once bisected by tramlines. Covered top cars first appeared on the MET in 1908. They quickly became popular with the travelling public.
D. Jones Collection

33

It is worth quoting from an article in the April 1909 issue of the *Tramway &* *Railway World* to illustrate some of the complexities – technical, administrative and financial – that had to be overcome in order to establish an electric tramway route in London. Rarely did the journal concentrate on just one seemingly minor part of the metropolitan tramway scene, but on this occasion the editor made an exception. One senses the frustration of those tramway advocates, including the author of the piece, which is headed:

Harrow Road Tramway. A Connecting Link In London's Tramway System.

In the year 1906, the Metropolitan Tramways Company purchased from the Harrow Road and Paddington Tramways Company, the horse tramway owned and worked by the latter company for a sum of £44,840. This price, of course, was paid for the tramway as a going concern, and included the Harrow Road line and also a short length of tramway in Chippenham Road from Harrow Road to the county boundary. The Metropolitan Tramways Company at once proceeded to electrify the Harrow Road line, and it was opened for traffic on the new system on October 10, 1906. Under the purchase clause of the Tramways Act the County Council determined last year to buy the part of the line within the county of London, but the Willesden Council consented to postpone purchasing the part in their district. The portion in London is 1.62 miles long, and for 0.58 mile of this distance one track is in London and the other in Willesden. By agreement the purchase price was fixed at £40,000. Last year also the company obtained Parliamentary powers to extend the line eastwards to Edgware Road near the Marble Arch, a distance of about a mile, on condition that the company should at once sell it to the County Council. The price, including expensive road widenings, was £52,152. Last month the Council confirmed a scheme put forward by the Highways Committee as the result of negotiations with the company, under which the company will exercise running powers over the old and new line, and will make a junction between the Council's Putney and Harlesden tramway and the Harrow Road line at the north end of Scrubs Lane. The Council will then have the option of running cars on the purchased lines or not.

. . . It appears from the figures published that the company will have to pay about 5d per car mile to the Council. If it is assumed that the working expenses of the company are 6d per car mile, then it will be necessary for the company to earn 11d per car mile, which is a high figure for such a route. If the Council do run cars on Harrow Road, the conditions are to be modified, and payments are to be made by the company in proportion to the ratio of mileage run by the company and the Council. In either event, the company will now have direct access from their extensive Middlesex system to the Marble Arch district, whence underground railways and omnibuses afford communication with most parts of London.

The total length of the Harrow Road tramway at present is 2.5 miles, all of double track, and the extension will bring this up to 3.5 miles. There are few gradients, and the steepest is of 1 in 29 for 200 ft. Curves are infrequent, and the radius of the sharpest is 140 ft. While the work of reconstruction with a view to electric working was in progress, very considerable street widenings had to be undertaken. These added the sum of £14,000 to the cost of the work. The narrowest width of the roadway is now 32 ft, so that in no place is the distance between the kerb and the rail less than the statutory 9ft 6ins.

. . . Cars belonging to the Metropolitan Electric Tramways Limited run over these lines in conjunction with lines leased to them by the Middlesex County Council.

On the partly completed route to Sudbury, car 92 stands at the temporary terminus by Iron Bridge, Stonebridge Park. The area was then quite rural and the Harrow Road was devoid of traffic.

Appended to this article was a plan and section of the track, which is illustrated here. The rest of the text deals at length with facts and figures concerning technical details of the track and electrical supply. However, aside from the jargon, one is left with the impression that the LCC struck a hard bargain for permission to encroach on its territory, all of which was hardly in the spirit of the recommendations of the 1905 Royal Commission. Such snail like progress on the tram front must have been greeted with glee by bus operators serving the area. Already, a 1904 survey had revealed the presence of 87 buses an hour on the Harrow Road. Omnibus companies also had the added advantage of being able to take their passengers into the heart of the West End. The tramlines finished short of the junction with the Edgware Road.

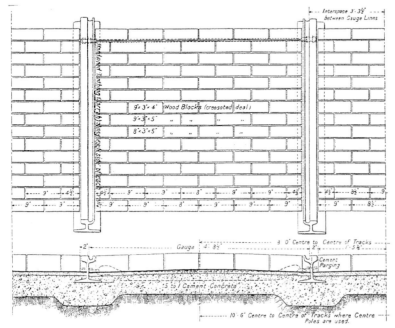

Plan and section of track, Harrow Road.

Plan and Section of Track—Harrow Road Tramways.

Car 216 stands just past the junction with the LCC lines at the College Park Hotel on the corner of Harrow Road and Scrubs Lane. Passengers transferring from MET trams could catch a connecting car over LCC metals south towards Shepherd's Bush, Hammersmith, Fulham and Putney. *D. Jones Collection*

In the event, the LCC's Scrubs Lane tramway opened on 30th May 1908 and a junction with the MET's Harrow Road line was ready for use on 25th April 1911. A short lived LCC service, in connection with the 1911 Coronation Exhibition at the White City, was operated from Putney via Hammersmith and the Harrow Road to Paddington. It was not a success and thereafter no regular LCC service ever traversed the section from Scrubs Lane to Paddington.

The last two routes in our survey of the MET's western lines connected North Finchley with Cricklewood, and Harlesden with Acton. On the line from North Finchley the tram tracks were set to commence in Ballards Lane at a junction with the link to Finchley Depot; they would then continue down Finchley Road to pass through Golders Green. This was once an isolated spot, devoid of much habitation, until a building boom was stimulated after the arrival of the Hampstead Tube on 22nd June 1907. The opening train was driven by the then President of the Board of Trade, David Lloyd George. This northern extension of the tube railway to what was only a green field site reflected the 'where the rails go, the houses will follow' philosophy of the Underground Electric Railways Company of London Limited. The same could be said for a number of the MET's lines that served quite sparsely populated areas; speculative builders were on the look-out for attractive locations situated on a tram route. Certainly, the inauguration of the electric tramway, on 16th December 1909, contributed to the success of Golders Green as an important transport interchange point.

Passenger service commenced on the section between Golders Green and Cricklewood Broadway on 21st February 1910. The complete route was now open and, for the first time, it was possible for all the Company's trams to reach the important repair and maintenance facilities at Hendon Depot. A glance at the map reveals

that beyond Golders Green the County Council built a spur, which diverged from the main line to serve a stub terminal at the county boundary in Childs Hill. The hope was that this short section of track would eventually be joined to an LCC tramway; however, this plan was to remain unfulfilled. The Childs Hill spur became, like its neighbour in Cricklewood, a rather useless appendage to a busy system. The one saving grace of the Childs Hill track was that it offered an emergency short working terminal, when the main road at Golders Green was congested.

The MET failure to connect with the LCC at Childs Hill and Cricklewood counts as a major disappointment. This story of missed opportunities was repeated at Acton, where the Company's rails ended in Horn Lane, a short distance from the London United main route from Shepherd's Bush to Uxbridge. The line from Harlesden was opened in two stages. Delays had been caused by extensive road works south of Willesden Junction, where the reconstruction of Victoria Road and its associated railway bridges had caused the contractor more problems than anticipated.

No celebrations took place when the line from Jubilee Clock, Harlesden to Willesden Junction Station opened on 30th June 1908. This must have disappointed some locals, because words were then exchanged with local county councillors, with the result that the inauguration of the completed tracks to Acton brought forth County Alderman Herbert Nield MP. With an official entourage on board, he piloted car 92 on the first journey from Willesden Junction to Horn Lane. Just to make sure everybody got their money's worth, County Alderman Charles Pinkham, Vice Chairman of the MCC's Light Railways and Tramways Committee, took the controls for the return journey to Harlesden. Full public service began the next day, 8th October 1909.

4. HERTFORD ROAD

Hertford Road has a long pedigree stretching back to the ancient Ermine Street that linked London to York. One of the early settlements along the road is Edmonton. Its most famous hostelry, the Bell Tavern, was immortalised by William Cowper (1731–1800) in his poem describing John Gilpin's ride to Ware. Whereas the hapless Gilpin had to hire a chaise and pair to reach the Bell from the City, travellers in the early nineteenth century had the option of using a daily coach service that departed from Bishopsgate. Matters had improved somewhat by the end of the century and, as we have seen, steam trams worked from Ponders End to Stamford Hill, where passengers transferred to horsecars in order to complete their journey through Stoke Newington, Dalston and Shoreditch to arrive at Norton Folgate, a stone's throw from the City of London.

The original Middlesex County Council plans envisaged an electric tramway that would traverse the county, linking LCC territory to Waltham Cross and Cheshunt in Hertfordshire. Although the route was paralleled by two steam railways, it was confidently assumed that the introduction of electric traction on the main road would generate lucrative short distance passenger traffic as well as attract commuters to London.

We know that the proud figure at the controls of car 42 was one W. Moore. The location is Waltham Cross, at the northern extremity of the system, just short of the Queen Eleanor Cross. *D. Jones Collection*

Type E car 148 is working from Bruce Grove to Alexandra Palace. The tram in the background is on the Hertford Road section. Single deckers in this part of the world were not a success and they were soon banished back to the environs of the Ally Pally, where they remained for the rest of their service lives.

The motorman of car 105 turns to check whether everyone is on board, before the conductor signals it is safe to start. On the left hand side of Fore Street is the famous Edmonton hostelry 'The Bell'.

The former North Metropolitan horsecar route as far as Tramway Avenue, Edmonton was owned by the MET outright; any extension northwards to the county boundary and beyond would be the property of the Middlesex and Hertfordshire county councils respectively. In the three years from 1905 to 1908 the goal of Waltham Cross was reached, but there the tracks ended. A probable reason for this curtailment can be found in the demands of Cheshunt Urban District Council for extensive and expensive road widening.

Significant progress on the Hertford Road section began on 22nd March 1905, when the tram service to Fore Street, Edmonton was extended to a crossover at Angel Bridge. Cars then ran from the new terminus to either Finsbury Park or Stamford Hill. That these vehicles had to be supplied by Wood Green Depot, thus adding an unwanted amount of dead mileage, was a source of frustration to the MET. Tramway officials must have been counting the days until Edmonton Depot became fully operational.

The last horsecar finally departed on 18th July 1905, and on the next day electric traction was inaugurated along the section between Angel Bridge and Tramway Avenue, Edmonton. Speed and weight restrictions applied to the bridge over the Great Eastern Railway at Lower Edmonton. The GER wanted the structure strengthened to support the new electric trams. A signalling system was adopted so that no two MET trams could be on the bridge at any one time. Maximum speed permitted was a very cautious 5mph (8km/h). A potential bottleneck was avoided at the southern approach to the bridge, when the Company constructed a siding in The Broadway, Lower Edmonton for vehicles terminating at Edmonton Town Hall. Reconstruction work was carried out by 1909, and the weight restrictions were then lifted.

Almost a year after the last horse tram entered Edmonton Depot, the MCC agreed a contract with Dick, Kerr & Co. for the building of track from Tramway Avenue to the quaintly named Freezy Water, just short of the Hertfordshire border. The Board of Trade inspection, on 26th November 1907, was carried out by Major Pringle, who was already well known to MET officials. The completed works were passed as satisfactory and the line opened to the public on 11th December. The same inspector returned to the area on 15th April 1908 for the completion of the line to Waltham Cross. Passenger service commenced two days later, on 17th April. The track ended within sight of the historic Eleanor Cross.

The network now assumed almost its final shape, but it still lacked several vital radial connections between the 'spokes of the wheel'. One of these links lay in an easterly direction towards Walthamstow via Ferry Lane. The other lay along Southbury Road from Ponders End to Enfield. Work on the latter began in the summer of 1909 and the tramway service was inaugurated on 20th February 1911 from Enfield GER Station to Ponders End. This was, as we shall see, the second electric tramway to reach Enfield. A line north of Winchmore Hill to the Market Place, Enfield Town had been opened on 1st July 1909.

Whilst plans for Southbury Road came to fruition, the Ferry Lane line never left the drawing board. The whole saga of the Tottenham to Walthamstow link can be characterised as so much energy being expended for no tangible result. Protracted deliberations between the interested parties dragged on for almost thirty years, before they were cut short by the arrival of the LPTB in 1933.

Unfortunately, the bad luck attending the Ferry Lane debacle seems also to have spread to part of the Southbury Road route. The gap between the two separate tramway termini in Enfield was destined never to be bridged. In spite of intensive

In this early view car 59 is working to Stamford Hill via Bruce Grove.

negotiations, the elected members of Enfield UDC stubbornly refused pressure by the county council to construct a connection between Southbury Road and Enfield Town Market Place, even a single track one. Again, narrow streets were cited as the cause of the problem. Whatever the reasons, the Ponders End to Enfield route was quickly relegated to a shuttle service; it was disparagingly referred to by the staff as the 'chicken run'.

At least the loss of status of one of the Enfield lines was not reflected in the trunk route linking the town with Manor House and Finsbury Park. Here prospects looked very bright indeed. The line north of the original Wood Green terminus was opened in stages. On 6th June 1907, trams were extended to Palmers Green, and on 1st August 1908, Winchmore Hill was reached. The County Council planners then paused for reflection. None of the conventional highways from Winchmore Hill to Enfield seemed suitable for tramway purposes. A decision was then made, in association with a local land developer, to construct a brand new thoroughfare across farmland. The road was eventually dubbed Ridge Avenue, and it carried a double track tramway. This was constructed by George Wimpey & Co. of Hammersmith, a firm which later achieved international fame as one of the world's major civil engineering concerns. However, at this stage of the company's existence, it was engaged in routine tram track laying and highway reconstruction work. The Winchmore Hill to Enfield contract was worth £40,220. Much correspondence in local newspapers was critical of the construction work necessary for the new tramway. It was claimed that the town, in the summer of 1908, was under siege from gangs of labourers and that businesses would suffer because local worthies could find no convenient places to leave their carriages, whilst the roadway was being dug up. Of course, most working people took the opposite point of view. Those who found travel expensive on the GER from Enfield Town, or who were put off using the Great Northern Railway's Enfield Chase Station, because of its bias towards a 'better class of passenger', welcomed the opportunity of sampling the new MET tram service. It was worth putting up with a bit of mess, if in the end they would get more miles for their pennies.

County Alderman Henry Burt was given charge of inaugural car 109, when it arrived at Enfield Town on the afternoon of Thursday, 1st July 1909. He and the official party had made the journey from Wood Green Depot. Contrary to what the carriage folk might have expected, large numbers of spectators turned up for the celebrations, and the triumphal progress of Enfield's first electric tram was greeted with cheers. No doubt, the news of a 2d (0.83p) workman's fare between Enfield and Wood Green brought forth an extra cheer from the assembled crowd at the Market Place. Business was brisk from 3rd July, when full public service commenced, and the line soon became one the MET's most profitable routes.

George Wimpey & Co. was again on hand, when contracts were let for the construction of the proposed link between Wood Green and North Finchley. Work began in 1906 and the first section along Bounds Green Road to a crossover opposite The Ranelagh Inn was opened on 28th November. Service was provided by single deck cars of Type E, which had been delivered from Brush of Loughborough in 1905. On 11th May 1907, these single deck tramcars were extended to a terminus by New Southgate Station. This was to remain the end of the line, until the link along Friern Barnet Road and Woodhouse Road to the Great North Road, North Finchley opened on 8th April 1909. In the meantime, the single deckers had been withdrawn, to be replaced by standard double deck cars.

42

A breakdown on the line can be one of the major drawbacks of any fixed track transport system. One hopes that these passengers eventually made it to Palmers Green without having to get off and walk. Power failures on the MET were rare, but they could potentially cause much inconvenience. Minor derailments could be rectified by reversing the car and then, by judicious use of a crowbar or a point iron, the errant vehicle could be coaxed back on the 'iron'. Inspectors were authorised to organise single track working to avoid any failed tramcar that was obstructing the right of way. *D. Jones Collection*

The delay in completion of the through route had been caused principally by a dispute between Friern Barnet UDC and the County Council over the narrow bridge that spanned the rails of the GNR just north of New Southgate Station. Added to this, there was further discord over the MCC's insistence that granite setts should be used instead of wood blocks in paving the new route. At this time, imported hardwood blocks of Australian Jarrah were considered the *ne plus ultra* of highway surfaces, and they were priced accordingly. Matters were settled on the bridge by using single track and on the main road by installing wood blocks between the tramlines and leaving macadam for the rest of the carriageway.

Electric trams opened up new transport links to communities such as New Southgate. The steam railway serving New Southgate Station would now face stiff competition. MET car 22 offered cheap fares and direct access to local shopping centres.

The western reserved track
ended by Priory Road. In
the 1930s the Alexandra
Palace was still offering a
range of activities, as listed
on the notice board next to
car 149; however, the
crowds associated with first
decade of the century had
drifted away. Tastes had
changed in popular culture.
The deluxe cinema was in
the ascendant. *D.W.K. Jones/
National Tramway Museum*

5. ALEXANDRA PALACE

Alexandra Palace lies perched atop a hill with fine views over the whole metropolitan area. Even though the Ally Pally, as the building is popularly known to Londoners, has its charms, it is still difficult to see how the place could justify three electric tramways, including the pioneer 1898 line, *and* a branch line terminus of the Great Northern Railway! In fact, from a twenty-first century perspective, when there are no rail connections from the area to the outside world, this overprovision of public transport seems positively extravagant in the extreme. Put bluntly, the two separate MET tram routes that once served Alexandra Palace were white elephants. They cannot be said to fit in with the rest of the network that was based on trunk and radial lines in suburban Middlesex, all of which had a good chance of being a financial success.

In the early 1900s one argument for the construction of a new tramway was probably based on the potential of Alexandra Palace as a leisure and entertainment centre. Since the opening of the park in July 1863 and the main building in May 1873, millions of Londoners had been drawn to the various attractions on offer. Aside from the delights of the zoo and its resident bears, the attractions included, within the walls of the palace, a range of activities such as garden shows, exhibitions, concerts, banquets, dances, lectures and sporting displays. There was also an indoor ice rink. Outside in the 180 acre (72.8 ha) park a grandstand looked over a race course, which had been opened in 1888. Non-horseracing types could exercise their skills on the golf course or on the boating lake. There were also seasonal events that included everything from athletics meetings to a daring demonstration of Victorian parachuting from a hot air balloon tethered above the grounds!

Another reason for building the tramway lay in the purchase of the estate by a group of local authorities, which included Middlesex County Council. The thinking was that a publicly owned amenity should be served by a transport system in which the ratepayers had an important stake. Hence, an application was submitted in 1901 for a Light Railways Order covering a proposed through route from Highgate to Wood Green via Muswell Hill and Alexandra Palace. Although this scheme had its merits, not everyone was convinced. Objections from local residents forced all interested parties to rethink the application. A shorter circular route became the preferred option, but even this ran into opposition, with result that the section along the South Terrace of the palace was vetoed. What remained was a patently unsatisfactory arrangement of two tram termini separated by the main palace building. At this juncture it was decided to go ahead with the truncated project, even though it later emerged that the Board of Trade would not permit double deck trams to work the routes. Only single deck vehicles would be allowed, because of the steep gradients

Some of the charm of the Alexandra Palace routes can be gauged by this picture taken some months before the end of tramway operation. In a scene almost devoid of humanity, car 148 trundles sedately towards the Muswell Hill gate on Priory Road. This view, one the author's favourites, truly evokes a lost world. *A.D. Packer Collection*

involved on the climb up to the palace. The existence of a low railway bridge that carried the GER Palace Gates branch over Station Road, Wood Green, also precluded double deck operation. Thus the crowd shifting potential of lines of double deckers, which had been clearly demonstrated at football matches, could not be realised during race meetings and gala events at the palace.

The line from the Wellington public house, Turnpike Lane to Muswell Hill and Alexandra Palace West was inspected by Major Pringle in November 1905 and opened for traffic on 6th December in the same year. The route from Muswell Hill Gate to the terminus was situated on private right of way. This form of segregated track was practically unknown in London, although it was used extensively on the Continent of Europe and in North America. In theory, since trams were unencumbered by other road users, they could achieve higher speeds, thus making the service more efficient. In practice, the Alexandra Palace West reserved track was never more than a mere novelty, and must therefore be considered an underused resource.

Service was initially provided on the short stretch from Turnpike Lane to Priory Road, Muswell Hill. Cars were extended to Alexandra Palace West as traffic dictated; eventually, as passengers failed to materialise, the service faded out to afternoons and evenings only. From October 1906 the focus shifted to the Priory Road section, when a new double deck service was inaugurated linking Muswell Hill to Finsbury Park. This was eventually to prove the only viable part of the line, and, as we shall see, Muswell Hill was later to be served by trunk route 51 to the City terminus at Aldersgate.

On the other side of the park, a new tramway connection from Wood Green to the palace featured a gradient of 1 in 10 (10%) on the Eastern Approach Road. Board of Trade regulations required trams to be fitted with mechanical track brakes and a 4 mph (6.4 km/h) speed limit was applied. The track brake had to be actuated at the start of the descent from the Alexandra Palace East terminus. Motormen assigned to this section would later be required to have at least two years' driving experience. Cars coming in the opposite direction were not allowed to make any stops on the uphill section. The first ceremonial vehicle to make the climb was driven by Sir Francis Cory-Wright at the formal opening, which took place on 9th April 1906. Sir Francis had begun his official journey at Bruce Castle. Service for the general public commenced two days later.

There was no reserved track on the eastern side of Alexandra Palace, although the rails on which car 141 is standing were laid in a private road owned by the park trustees. In this view the crowds have departed. Lack of passengers contributed to the poor financial results of the two Ally Pally services.

The initial optimism concerning the Alexandra Palace routes soon evaporated when the passenger figures were analysed. Steps were taken to vary the itinerary of the tram services in an effort to generate more traffic. Through cars were first introduced between Alexandra Palace East and Bruce Grove, Tottenham, but they were quickly withdrawn, as there were said to be operational difficulties in running single and double deckers together along most of the route. A similar fate awaited another attempt at a mixed service, this time from the eastern terminus to Finsbury Park. There seemed to be no solution to the problem. The MET decided to make the best of a bad job and retain two distinct shuttle services, which would only require a maximum of 10 single deck trams.

On the western approach the segregated reserved track was more reminiscent of North America than North London. Usually British tramway operators liked to stick to public highways. After the demise of the trams in 1938 this private right of way was incorporated into a road for all vehicular traffic.

In spite of the nightmare financial situation, or maybe because of it, the Alexandra Palace single deckers entered into local folklore. John Barrie in his 1969 lecture notes entitled *North London Tramways* has written affectionately of the Ally Pally Bang Bangs. The rhyming slang term 'the Ally Pally Bread and Jam' was recalled by the present author's grandparents. Some people also referred rather facetiously to the Ally Pally Rockets in acknowledgement of the snail's pace with which they crept downhill from the palace. The sad expression 'as empty as an Ally Pally tram' also had some currency amongst North London folk.

Somehow, the little single deckers seemed to develop a mythology all of their own. They were, of course, different from almost all the other trams operating in London and the Home Counties, because they didn't have an 'upstairs'. This lack of outside seating probably led to their being called continental trams or colonial cars. In fact the latter term was spot on, when four of the Type E single deckers were sold to Auckland, New Zealand in 1907. However, during special events at the palace they could come into their own. They might be packed with young people going to a dance or they could help transport a more sedate gathering of classical music buffs. Sometimes, as many as 12,000 concert goers would turn up for one of the famous organ recitals. According to a 1910 guidebook, the park gates usually opened at 10am and the palace an hour later. At Bank Holidays and on certain special days, a charge of sixpence (2.5p) was levied to sample the attractions on offer in the park grounds – children got in half price. This entry fee was collected on the tram as it passed through the park gate.

After the fine summer days had passed and the gloom of winter had descended on the place, the grim reality was often that tram crews could easily outnumber passengers. In cold weather the motorman had precious little protection from the elements. It goes without saying that there were no heaters inside the cars, so the conductor suffered almost as much as his colleague on the open driving platform. The plight of tramway personnel obliged to work in near sub-zero temperatures was related by John Barrie (*op cit*), when he quoted a story related to him by a former conductor.

When the weather was bad during winter, the single deck tramcars used to rush as fast as they dared from the palace to the Wellington and back. The few minutes layover thus obtained could be spent by the crews in warming themselves round a brazier or an open fire at the Alexandra Palace West terminus. The end of the track was situated next to the Great Northern Railway (later LNER) station. If firewood was in short supply, then it was supplemented by coal provided courtesy of the GNR. Motormen and conductors used to make gestures and pull faces at the engine drivers, who would then return the complement by lobbing pieces of coal in the direction of the tram crews! Thus, at the risk of being knocked out by a rogue lump of Welsh anthracite, the fuel supply for the MET staff fire was maintained.

This sporting ritual probably took place almost unnoticed by members of the public. One wonders if the GNR could actually afford to subsidise the opposition with free fuel, especially in view of the fact that trains on the Highgate to Alexandra Palace branch often ran with few passengers. A depressing pattern was set when the steam railway line opened on 24th May 1873, failed to achieve success, and closed some weeks later on 1st August. It then lay dormant for two years before beginning a cycle of intermittent service to the palace. A plan in the late 1930s to electrify the railway as part of an extended Northern Line was suspended due to the Second World War and was subsequently scrapped, leaving the line to expire quietly on 3rd July 1954.

This postcard illustrates some of the delights to be had on a day out in the Palace Grounds, Alexandra Park. By the end of the Edwardian era, donkey rides and horse racing are much in evidence. The famous bears have obviously been given their marching orders. Many visitors would arrive by tram, as illustrated by car 134, which stands at the eastern terminus.

Back on the tram front, the two Ally Pally routes lingered on in a sort of tramway twilight zone, until they were jolted out of their stupor by the declaration of hostilities in 1914. The opening weeks of the First World War saw all kinds of upheavals. The cavalry requisitioned the palace grounds, then pandemonium broke out when the horses stampeded; the military was subsequently sent packing. Next up on the visitors' list was a party of Belgian refugees. Many were conveyed by tram to temporary accommodation in the palace. Unconfirmed reports suggest that, amongst the procession of single deck cars, there were at least two Type D open top double deckers. What the Board of Trade inspector would have thought of this violation of safety regulations is not recorded. However, it is almost certain that this was a unique occurrence.

The palace and grounds were officially closed to normal service trams from 11th September 1914 to 30th March 1920, although exceptions were made, as in the transportation of the Belgians. Later in the war the enemy did succeed in occupying the park, albeit under Allied armed guard. German and Austrian civilian internees were housed in the area and some were set to work in the palace grounds. The sense of isolation and the derelict state of the tramways gets several mentions in accounts written by inmates of the POW camp. One of the best was published under the title *Dreizehn Monate hinter dem Stacheldraht* (13 months behind barbed wire) by Otto Schimming.

After the park was reopened to the public, sections of the tram track were found to be in a poor state. A collision between two trams at the foot of the Eastern Approach Road added to the Company's distress. Further financial discomfort was caused by the continuing deficit accrued by the lines. These circumstances ruled out any modernisation programme and both the Alexandra Palace routes remained almost unchanged throughout the rest of the life of the MET.

On Station Road, Wood Green, it is clear to see why only single deckers were allowed on this section of track. The bridge in the picture carries the former Great Eastern Railway branch to Palace Gates. The trams were replaced by buses in February 1938 and the last passenger train left Palace Gates Station in January 1963. *C. Klapper/Omnibus Society*

49

6. Capital Connections

The 1905 Royal Commission had already stated the pressing need for metropolitan tramway operators to put aside their differences and come to sensible arrangements in respect of through services and integrated fares. There was a uniform track gauge in the London area; therefore, no great technical difficulties could be claimed in support of isolationism. In theory, rails separated by a gap of a few feet could be easily joined. However, the founding fathers of the LCC electric tramways had an aversion to overhead wires. They adopted the underground conduit system of current collection and it was the conduit that faced the MET across the county boundary at Highgate Archway Tavern, Finsbury Park and Stamford Hill.

After expending much effort in the 1906–08 North London electrification programme, the sheer cost of conduit construction did eventually make the LCC come to its senses. The Scrubs Lane route, which connected to the MET's Harrow Road line, was equipped for overhead trolley operation. Obviously the next step for the LCC engineers was to devise a practical and mechanically sound way of ensuring a smooth transition from conduit to overhead equipped tracks. The first change pits were employed in South London from November 1908. Trams were then able to pick up and discard their conduit ploughs in a relatively simple fashion. Cars working on through services had to possess both plough and overhead trolley gear.

There were now few, if any, technical problems in the way of joint MET/LCC services. The benefits to passengers of not having to change trams at the county boundary seemed self evident. Top covers on the tramcars had made travel on the outside much less of an inconvenience in bad weather. Cheap fares were also an attractive feature of tramway travel. Frustratingly, both county councils were still inclined to dally, until the impact of motor bus competition became apparent. The famous London General B-type bus was in the final stages of development by the autumn of 1910 and in the following year it had begun to make an impact on the streets. Seven years later, after the end of the First World War, there were over 2,000 B-types, ready to plug the gaps in the tramway network and to offer potential passengers an alternative to the tramcar.

The first small step towards through running came with the publication in 1908 of the LCC's *London Tramways Guide*. Over 130 pages were devoted to describing main landmarks and places of interest. The general idea was to encourage the public to go out and about by tramcar in their capital city. Route maps indicated the principal connections to MET services. In the following year, LCC cars working from central London termini were furnished with side destination boards informing passengers where they had to change in order to continue their journey into Middlesex.

St John Street, Smithfield, on the very edge of the City of London, is traditionally regarded as the start of the Great North Road. The Windmill, on the right, marks the site from which the St Albans coaches once began their journeys. A somewhat more modern conveyance is MET car 289 on route 79. The City authorities firmly objected to trams, so this was the furthest that the tracks were allowed to come.

Stamford Hill was one of the locations in London where overhead wires met the conduit. Tramcars from the LCC and MET face one another across a railless gap of a few yards. The crew of car 65 are getting ready to take their charge back to Wood Green. On the London side of the road junction two standard LCC Class E cars await passengers who have transferred from the MET tram.

By the time of the 1911 *London Tramways Guide*, the LCC had already concluded through running agreements with several East London municipal systems. Trams were now travelling uninterrupted from Aldgate to Epping Forest and Ilford Broadway. On the south side of the Thames in Woolwich, Bexley Council trams could be seen on LCC owned tracks in Beresford Square. Progress in these areas meant that mutually beneficial arrangements could now be brokered between neighbouring tramway operators.

However, just as everything seemed set fair for an agreement between the LCC and the MET, a dose of rather petty parochialism threatened to derail matters. A dispute blew up that delayed through running for almost two years. The LCC wished to purchase the existing electric tramway from Manor House to Finsbury Park and then relay it as conduit track. Not surprisingly, several local authorities, the Metropolitan Police and the MET Board regarded this proposal as a retrograde step. Notes were passed between the two tramway operators and it took time for a compromise to be reached. The upshot of the negotiations was that a temporary change pit was constructed at Finsbury Park, pending the completion of new conduit track along Seven Sisters Road to a permanent change pit at Manor House. Overhead wires for shortworking MET cars were retained as far as Finsbury Park.

The Finsbury Park to Manor House boundary tramway was sold to the LCC on 17th July 1912. Thereafter, affairs moved quickly. On 1st August 1912 a through service between Enfield and Euston Road was inaugurated. The first tram to leave central London for Enfield was LCC car 1602. This vehicle had been hired by the MET along with other members of the E/1 Class 1590–1604. Although this motive power loan was a temporary expedient, the legal niceties were observed and the large gold letters LCC on the waist panel of each car were replaced by MCC. These trams were kept at Wood Green Depot until August 1915, when they were eventually returned to their owner.

Preparations were put in hand for the equipping of MET cars with plough carriers, so that they could operate over conduit tracks. The trend was very much in favour of top covered bogie cars with maximum traction trucks. In this field the LCC had already set the standard pattern for the London tramcar with its E and E/1 vehicles. Interestingly, the MET had been ahead of the game, when they specified that all tramcars ordered after February 1908 should have Mountain & Gibson maximum traction trucks, which could easily be fitted with plough gear.

Further talks with the LCC resulted in additional agreements in respect of joint services. A straightforward system of route numbering had been introduced from

Through running between the MET and the LCC brought benefits to both parties. LCC Class E/1 car 1592 is pictured here at Wood Green, probably during its loan spell to the Metropolitan Electric. From this angle it is impossible to tell whether the letters MCC have been affixed to the side of the tram. Type A car 85 heads north for Finchley, whilst another MET open top tram waits at the terminus in Lordship Lane.
D. Jones Collection

LCC conduit tracks are to be seen in the foreground of this view of Highgate Archway Tavern. The change pit from conduit to overhead is just to the right of the policeman.
D. Jones Collection

autumn 1912 – even numbers for South London services, odd numbers for north of the Thames. At this juncture it is worth remembering that there were still some subtle differences in the language used by the two organisations. Hence, an observer standing at Finsbury Park could record an MET *Type* H car on *route* 79, followed by a standard LCC *Class* E/1 car on *service* 21! Luckily, minor semantic quibbles did not hinder the establishment, on 1st March 1913, of service 27 – Seven Sisters Corner to Euston Road, and service 59 – Edmonton Town Hall to Holborn. Later in the year, on 23rd June, service 79 was inaugurated between Waltham Cross and Smithfield Market. This route was subsequently to become a favourite with excursionists and hikers wishing to gain access to the countryside. The journey out to Waltham Cross, with a through fare of sixpence (2.5p), took just over one hour and a quarter.

As expected, passenger levels and fare receipts rose, therefore confirming the success of the new policy. The LCC *Map & Guide to Services, November 1913* proudly announced a further route, numbered 51, which ran from Muswell Hill to Bloomsbury via Green Lanes and Essex Road. Cars on service 21, which departed from the central London terminus at Holborn, Grays Inn Road, were extended past Finsbury Park on 23rd November 1913. The route now went via Wood Green and New Southgate to terminate at North Finchley, Tally Ho Corner.

In the late spring of 1914 construction work began at Archway Tavern on a new junction and rail link in the Great North Road services. On 24th September 1914, after completion of the change pit, service 9 from Moorgate was prolonged to High Barnet, and service 19 trams from Euston Road now ended their journey at North Finchley. Vehicle allocations varied on the joint routes. The official policy declared

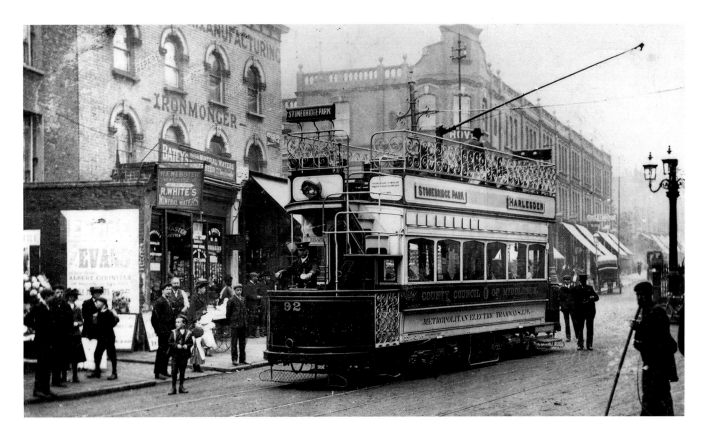

that services 29 to Enfield and 31 to Palmers Green, together with services 21, 59 and 79, were worked by cars of both operators. LCC Class E/1 trams ran on service 9, whilst the MET had sole possession of services 51 and 19. In practice, these arrangements were fluid. Recent research has indicated that the MET and the LCC frequently readjusted the ratio of cars on joint services so as to equalise running expenses.

Physical connections between the two tram systems were only one element of the story. Discussions had been going on behind the scenes. They were aimed at making the Metropolitan Electric Tramways part of a larger and more efficient public transport network. As early as April 1902, the *BET Monthly Gazette* had announced the formation of an Automobile Committee to keep watch on developments in internal combustion engine technology. By 1906 the company's rail based activities had reached a high water mark. In the succeeding years tramway promotion no longer promised such lucrative returns. At the time of the British Electric Traction Company's AGM in 1911 the threat from the motor bus had become so acute that several important shareholders pressed the Chairman to mobilise the company's resources in order to run fleets of motor vehicles. This disquiet must have filtered down to the MET board, because a new organisation – The Tramways (MET) Omnibus Company Limited – was registered on 13th January 1912. An initial order for one hundred buses was placed; the bodies were to be built by Brush of Loughborough, with Daimler supplying each chassis. The idea behind this purchase of a bus fleet was to develop new bus routes and feeder services to the existing tramways.

A quirk of history meant that MET trams working the Harrow Road service through High Street, Harlesden, would penetrate deep into LCC territory. This through running arrangement in West London stayed out of the limelight. Paddington was the only central London tram terminus not to be equipped for conduit operation. *D. Jones Collection*

Events now began to move swiftly. In February 1912, the Underground Electric Railways Company of London Ltd (later referred to as 'the Combine') acquired a majority holding in the London General Omnibus Company. Principal movers in the negotiations were the banker, Sir Edgar Speyer and the Managing Director of the Combine, Albert Stanley (later Lord Ashfield). The Combine already owned the London United Tramways, and it was probably no great surprise when the MET announced on 17th July 1912 that it was in talks with the LUT about a link up.

A new group called the London and Suburban Traction Company was subsequently registered to cover the operations of both the LUT and the MET. In May 1913, the South Metropolitan Electric Tramways & Lighting Company, which operated lines in the Croydon area, was absorbed into the London and Suburban. The Southmet (SMET), as it was popularly known, was the BET's last major tramway holding in London. To all intents and purposes, the London and Suburban existed only on paper; however, it was in fact a full member of the Combine.

This grouping into one large public transport organisation was trumpeted by the public relations people as promising economies of scale, plus many extra benefits for travellers. Immediate practical advantages from the merger included through tickets for passengers transferring from MET trams to tube trains at Golders Green and Highgate. The MET's brand new motor bus operation was integrated into the London General network, and the spectre of damaging bus competition with the LGOC along tram routes was lifted.

Many county councillors, both in Middlesex and London, were caught unprepared by the speed of these changes. Of course, the MET already had binding agreements with Middlesex County Council and these had to be honoured. The tramway company also relied on the goodwill of the London County Council in the matter of joint services. However, a potential conflict of interests was alleviated by the fact that majority control of both county councils rested with groups broadly sympathetic to the Conservative Party. Therefore, the consensus on through running and the public/private partnership in the MET was maintained. Elected representatives on the political left were moved to wonder whether the new arrangements constituted a 'capitalist stitch up' and, as such, posed a real threat to the rest of London's municipally owned tramways. Leader of the London Labour Party, Herbert Morrison, who was subsequently Minister of Transport in the 1929–1931 Labour Government and Deputy to Prime Minister Clement Attlee from 1945–51, was never in any doubt. He referred to 'Lord Ashfield and his wicked combine' in his 1933 book, entitled *Socialisation and Transport*.

The Combine's involvement with the three tramways of the London and Suburban Traction Company also invited a degree of scepticism from other quarters. The fact that the MET, LUT and Southmet were regarded as separate from the Common Fund Group effectively prevented the profitable bus and tube side of the undertaking from subsidising the ailing tramways. At least, this is what the shareholders were given to understand. Critics of the Combine, of whom there were many, muttered darkly about financial legerdemain and disingenuous statements from the Chairman and some of the board members. John Cliff, one time Assistant General Secretary of the Transport & General Workers' Union and later a respected member of the London Transport Executive, maintained that Lord Ashfield was always keen to avoid labour disputes because any subsequent enquiry might unearth to both shareholders and senior staff embarrassing facts about financial irregularities.

LONDON UNDERGROUND GROUP OF UNDERTAKINGS

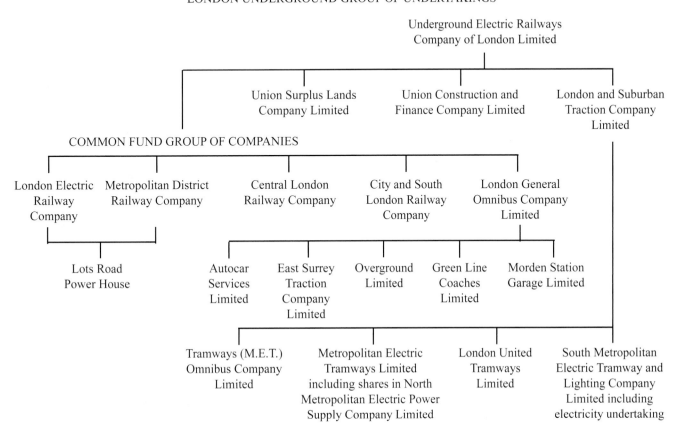

Underground Electric Railways
Company of London Limited

Union Surplus Lands
Company Limited

Union Construction and
Finance Company Limited

London and Suburban
Traction Company
Limited

COMMON FUND GROUP OF COMPANIES

London Electric
Railway
Company

Metropolitan District
Railway Company

Central London
Railway Company

City and South
London Railway
Company

London General
Omnibus Company
Limited

Lots Road
Power House

Autocar
Services
Limited

East Surrey
Traction
Company
Limited

Overground
Limited

Green Line
Coaches
Limited

Morden Station
Garage Limited

Tramways (M.E.T.)
Omnibus Company
Limited

Metropolitan Electric
Tramways Limited
including shares in North
Metropolitan Electric Power
Supply Company Limited

London United
Tramways
Limited

South Metropolitan
Electric Tramway and
Lighting Company
Limited including
electricity undertaking

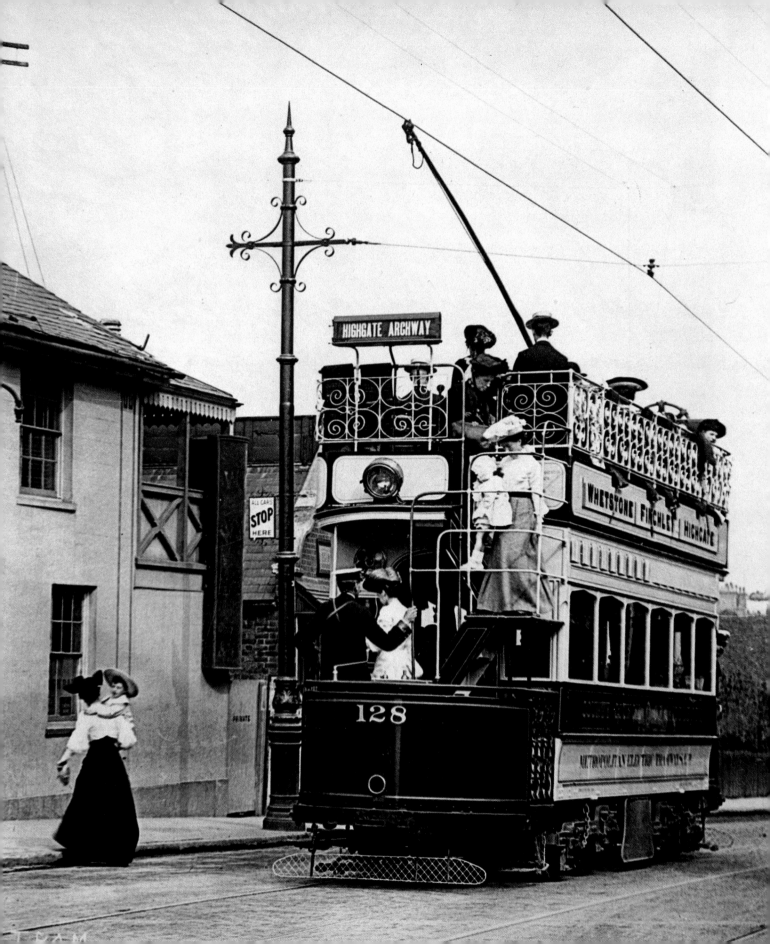

7. TRAMCARS

At the beginning of the twentieth century trams were built to last. Sound materials, seasoned hard woods, solid construction techniques, tried and tested electrical equipment, plus well engineered running gear all contributed to a vehicle which could stand up to the stresses and strains of transporting Londoners. However, once in possession of such a reliable product, it was easy to resist the temptation to modernise and not to tinker with the fabric of the vehicle. These very qualities of durability were seized on by critics in the 1920s and 1930s. Outdated design and hard wooden seats were decidedly unattractive when matched against new buses and trolleybuses. Pneumatic tyres, advanced suspension and upholstered seats offered by the competition gave passengers a smoother ride.

To be fair to the company, there were improvements made to traditional rolling stock; the MET was well aware of the image it was projecting to the public. It was also concerned that vehicles used on joint services with the LCC matched their inner London sisters in performance. Covered tops, improved braking, more powerful motors, enclosed platforms and transverse seating were eventually seen as fundamental to establishing a renovated fleet. In short, the MET modernisation programme was carried out in stages.

In the Ministry of Transport returns for the financial year 1928–29, the MET was listed as having 313 cars in stock, at an average of 68.88 seats per car! Obviously, since not everyone could squeeze on to a seat, accommodation had to be found on each tram for numbers of standing passengers. These straphangers went some way to contribute to the 108 million passenger total for the year. The Ministry figures for this period are significant in that they mark the last full year of the traditional MET fleet, as described in this chapter. The watershed came in May 1929 with the introduction of the first prototypes of the revolutionary new Feltham cars.

Two vehicles – car 318, Bluebell and car 319, Poppy – fall outside the traditional category of London tramcars. They have been allocated a section to themselves at the end of the chapter.

Aside from the grouping of the fleet into classes or types of vehicle, there was a further division for accounting purposes between county and Metropolitan Electric cars. Trams wholly owned and paid for by the MET were instantly recognisable by the fact that they did not bear the name of the county council on their waist panels. They were originally put to work on sections of the former North Metropolitan Company from Finsbury Park to Wood Green and Edmonton, after they had been reconstructed for electric traction. Trams allocated to the Harrow Road line also came into this category.

Type A tramcar 128 dating from 1906, on the Barnet to Archway route.

Cars ordered for the county council and charged against the MET/MCC joint account had to be approved by members of the MCC's Light Railways & Tramways Committee. A similar situation existed in Hertfordshire, although the number of trams was minuscule, there being only short sections of track on HCC territory in Barnet and Waltham Cross. Originally, five trams – cars 159, 161, 162, 163 and 164 were lettered COUNTY COUNCIL OF HERTFORDSHIRE. In later years, only Type C/1 cars 207 and 208 belonged to the select Hertfordshire group.

Unless stated otherwise in the text, all vehicles survived until 1st July 1933 to be incorporated into the London Transport fleet. Under the new regime rolling stock repair and maintenance work continued at Hendon Depot. Scrapping of ex-MET vehicles began with Type B cars and ended in January 1939 when members of the last batch of Type G and H met the breaker's torch. The symbol (II) indicates a second series car that took the fleet number of an earlier vehicle.

Lettered COUNTY COUNCIL OF HERTFORDSHIRE, car 208 rests on home territory, at Barnet Church, before crossing Middlesex and the County of London to reach Tottenham Court Road terminus on route 19. *D. Jones Collection*

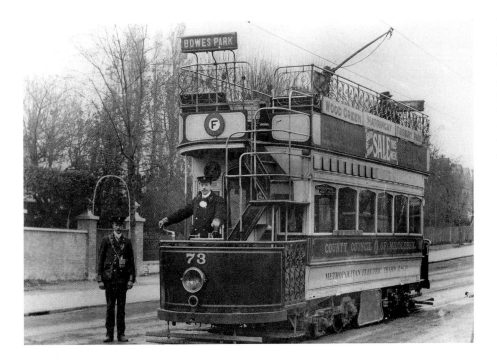

Type A. Cars 71–130

These vehicles were based on a design introduced to the streets of Middlesex by the London United Tramways. It seems that the county councillors from Middlesex had strong, conservative views on what style of tramcar would best serve their interests. Frequent visits and official missives to the Brush works at Loughborough resulted in several changes of specification. Delays were caused by sometimes quite minor matters, like the type of floor matting to be employed in the lower saloon.

In essence the Type A trams were already outdated, when delivered from Brush in 1905/6. In spite of the old fashioned look, a touch of elegance was conveyed by the elaborate wrought iron scrollwork that lined the upper deck above the decency boards. Access to the 38 outside wooden seats was via two Robinson type split staircases; the open top, especially in inclement weather, offered Spartan accommodation regarded as suitable for working men and smokers. The uncanopied body also gave precious little protection to the motorman on the driving platform.

Things were more refined on the bottom deck, where the ratepayers of Middlesex could judge how wisely their money had been invested. Examples of late Victorian/ early Edwardian furnishing style were revealed after passing through double sliding doors, which led into the lower saloon. Inside the vehicle, under a bird's eye maple wood clerestory ceiling, adorned with six cut glass light fittings, each shaped in the form of a pineapple, were two long bench seats with space for 32 passengers. Cushions of old gold Utrecht velvet, backed with leather, were placed on the seats, but they quickly became soiled with use and had to be dispensed with. The same fate awaited the coconut fibre mats that were laid on the lower deck floor. Dark brown curtains, attached to poles by the six windows on each side of the car, could be pulled back in the day time and tied up. The curtains were obviously made of durable material, because they outlived the cushions and the floor mats; most survived until the end of the Edwardian era.

Each vehicle of Type A was equipped with two BTH B18 controllers linked to two 28hp motors; there was a single motor for each Brush Type BB maximum traction bogie. This motor configuration soon proved to be a mistake, as the cars were slow and distinctly underpowered. Trucks were in the reversed position, with the smaller pony wheels leading. Rheostatic and hand brakes were originally supplied as standard, but by 1916 all members of this type had been fitted with magnetic track brakes. The position of the headlamp varied. Cars delivered earlier had a dash mounted lamp. Later it was decided to move the lamp to a position on the canopy above the motorman's head. Some vehicles had headlights in both positions.

Although officially frowned upon by the LCC, open top cars 73, 80, 88, 92, 113 and 118 were fitted with conduit gear in 1920 and they were used on joint services. They presented a rather anachronistic spectacle amongst all the LCC's standard covered top cars. In fact, one suspects that the MET management was probably shamed into ordering two batches of top covers for the remaining open toppers. They were manufactured by the LGOC at Chiswick Works. When in service, trams fitted with these top covers gave a distinct impression of having had the upper decks grafted on as a sort of afterthought. The best that could be said of them was that their tall and ungainly appearance stood out in contrast to other highway users.

A better result was achieved with car 77. This one off conversion earned the soubriquet 'The Silver Queen'. The fully enclosed top deck was surmounted by a domed roof that was painted an aluminium colour. Direct quarter turn stairs replaced the Robinson variety, and upholstered seating was supplied for the lower deck. Electrical equipment was updated and two 50hp motors were installed. It should be noted that higher powered motors had also been fitted to other members of Type A.

Five trams of this type failed to make the transition to London Transport ownership in 1933. The rest were renumbered in the LT 2413–2447 and 2448–2466 series. 'The Silver Queen' received the new fleet number 2412 and was scrapped along with the last remnants of MET Type A in September 1936.

Many British tramways continued to rebuild older cars when they should have turned to more modern vehicles. The MET did have the Felthams, but they also stuck with trams from the opening days of the network. London Transport car 2436 is formerly MET Type A car 111 and would survive in this form until February 1936. In spite of the covered top deck, the motorman is still unprotected from the elements.

Type B. Cars 1–35, 36–70

These vehicles, wholly owned by the MET, entered service before the Middlesex cars of Type A. They were open top bogie cars with seating for 30 people inside and 38 outside. Cars 36–70 had both bench and transverse seats in the bottom deck. This reduced the seating capacity in the lower saloon to 24. Both batches had similar brake, electrical and running gear to their sister vehicles in Type A. A full canopy over the driving platforms gave the motorman some protection from the elements.

Internal furnishings were less opulent than those on cars 71–130, but then the MET's parent company, the BET, consisted of hard headed businessmen, not county councillors out to impress the voters – in line with this policy, long lasting woven rattan cane and not velvet cushions covered the two-and-one transverse seats in cars 36–70! This latter batch received the classification Type B/1.

In line with official policy, vehicles were equipped in the early 1920s with more modern controllers and upgraded motors. Withdrawal of the class began in 1926, when cars 2, 12, 31 and 46 were relegated to the breakdown fleet. As the new Feltham cars were delivered, more Type B trams fell by the wayside and there were only 24 left when the MET fleet was incorporated into London Transport. The LT series 2498–2521 was reserved for this type, but some cars were scrapped before they could be repainted. At the end of 1935 Type B was extinct.

Cars 3, 4, 5, 7, 9, 10, 11, 13, 15, 16, 19, 24, 26, 27, 30 and 34 were sent to Hendon Works in 1912–1916 for conversion into top covered, open balcony trams. Unfortunately, the new model, thus created, lacked much in elegance. The Type B/2 cars, as they were called, looked ungainly and top heavy. Their one redeeming quality was that the use of higher powered motors compensated for the extra weight. Drivers handling the new B/2s on the Harrow Road routes were said to be pleased with their performance. On passing into the LPTB fleet, they gained the numbers 2467–2482, and the last was scrapped in the spring of 1936.

Type B car 48 was part of the original BET fleet; hence it did not bear any Middlesex markings. Local businesses were quick to take advantage of the advertising space offered by the tramcars.

When the Type B vehicles were upgraded, they received top covers with this rather irregular window arrangement. From an aesthetic viewpoint, the two decks seem to be ill matched.

Type C car 164 is seen at High Road, Finchley in the early days of the system. These handsome looking vehicles must have made quite an impact on a travelling public used to horse buses and suburban steam trains. *D. Jones Collection*

Type C. Cars 151–165

These trams were built by Brush in 1906. They were open top bogie cars with direct quarter turn stairs leading to an upper deck that seated 42 people. Two longitudinal bench seats in the lower saloon could accommodate a maximum of 32 passengers. Electrical equipment and running gear was similar to that used on types A and B. Conversion of all fifteen cars to Type C/2 followed in 1912–1916. They received new top covers with open balconies and were fitted with 40hp motors and Westinghouse magnetic brakes. In the late 1920s they were upgraded with more powerful motors and new controllers. After transfer to the LPTB they were renumbered in the series 2483–2497 and most were disposed of in the summer of 1936.

Type C/1. Cars 192–211

To all intents and purposes these trams had much in common with cars 151–165; however, they differed in the form of truck they used. Mountain & Gibson Type 3L maximum traction trucks, with the pony wheels facing inwards in the normal position, similar to those employed under LCC cars, were adopted. Further LCC influence was demonstrated by the fact that one of the bogies under each car could be easily adapted to receive a conduit plough carrier. These were fitted from 1912–1916 and the original 28hp motors were replaced by ones rated at 40hp.

Cars 192–211 were rebuilt with all enclosed top covers, constructed at Chiswick in 1929. Due to height restrictions under the railway bridge at Turnpike Lane, these cars and those of Type G were the only double deckers allowed to pass underneath. At the time of modernisation the original seating layout was updated and transverse seats were substituted in the lower saloon. The cars received the LT fleet numbers 2282–2301 and the last one perished in the summer of 1938.

Type D. Cars 166–191

These vehicles were classic open top trams of a type that could be seen in towns and cities throughout the UK. Built by Brush in 1906, each car had seats for 22 inside and 32 outside, and ran on a single four wheel truck of six feet (1828mm) wheelbase. After the First World War trucks were lengthened in order to receive a plough carrier, so that cars could work over LCC conduit lines. Car 191 was a one off, being allocated to class D/1. It predated the rest of the group by three years, having been manufactured by Brush as a sample vehicle for the approval of new buyers. Until the early 1920s it could easily be identified because it had three side windows instead of the normal four of the rest of the type.

At the end of their useful life in 1931 most Type D cars were scrapped, although five (including car 191) were transferred to the works fleet.

Type D car 170 has the county crest on the rocker panel underneath the gold lettered METROPOLITAN fleet name. Much to the LCC's disgust, this car was equipped with conduit equipment, so that it could work joint services into central London. The LCC rightly regarded such single truck, open top designs as distinctly 'passé' and not at all what was needed to improve the image of the tramways. *A.B. Cross collection*

In July 1924, Type E car 141 takes a rest from its Ally Pally duties to pose for the official photographer. Note the prominent dark green and white LIPTON'S TEA advertisement. In theory, advertising revenue was meant to pay for any repainting work needed to keep each vehicle looking smart. In those days it was considered a sackable offence to send any tram out on the road in a dirty or grimy state! *LT Museum*

Type E. Cars 131–150

In many ways these were the most distinctive vehicles the company owned, before the arrival of the Felthams. They were the Ally Pally cars – single deckers running on four wheel Brush Radial trucks of 8ft 6ins (2590mm) wheelbase. The saloon of each tram was originally divided by double sliding doors into two compartments. The smokers had 12 seats and those wishing to avoid the nicotine fug were confined to a space for 24 people. In practice, the Metropolitan Police, as the licensing authority, objected to any smoking on the cars and the partitions were quickly dismantled.

Headlamps were fitted to the roof above the motorman. They were subsequently removed, but by the late 1920s they had reappeared mounted on the dashes. In 1907 cars 135, 136, 143 and 144 were shipped out to the BET owned system of Auckland in the North Island of New Zealand. Sister cars 145 and 150 made a somewhat less exotic trip over to the SMET in Croydon, where they stayed for three years from 1920. Car 132 was seriously damaged in an accident on Easter Monday 1920. It was rebuilt as a one man operated tram with a front entrance/exit. However, the authorities baulked at the suggestion that the car could be used on the gradient up to Alexandra Palace. Since it then had no future with the MET, car 132 was transferred to work on LUT lines in Kingston. It was renumbered 341 by the London United.

Some members of Type E found themselves used on departmental duties and they could be seen ferrying around goods and chattels between depots. Car 146 doubled as a snow plough on the rare occasions when drifts threatened to cut off the palace from the outside world. It also had the honour of being decorated for the Wood Green Charter celebrations.

Very much the unsung heroines of the fleet, the usefulness of the little single deckers came to an end when the Alexandra Palace routes closed on 23rd February 1938. The last fifteen single deckers, numbered 2302–2316 in the LT series, then made their journeys to the scrapyard.

As described in the text, several Type E cars found themselves delegated to the Surrey/Kent border on South Metropolitan duties. All reference to Middlesex County Council has been erased from the waist panel. Although this may have been a purely legal matter, one suspects that the niceties of London's tribal allegiances had to be observed! *W. Gratwicke*

Car 146 is depicted after passing into London Transport ownership. It has been decorated for Wood Green Charter Day. Before the end of the Alexandra Palace routes in February 1938, anecdotal reports suggest that at least one Type E tram was used by the pioneering BBC television service as a mobile test rig for outside broadcast equipment. *LT Museum*

Type F. Cars 212–216

These vehicles reflected the influence of the standard LCC E/1 tram on MET thinking. They were the system's first bogie cars with an all-enclosed top deck. Seating was for 32 passengers in the lower saloon and for 46 on the upper deck. A headlamp was positioned in the canopy bend above the driving platform. Transverse upholstered seats were later fitted to the lower deck and all five trams took part in the upgrading programme of new motors and electrical equipment. At the end of the MET era, cars 214 and 216 were further modernised by the installation of new dashes and driver's windscreens. The five trams became London Transport cars 2256–60; they were withdrawn from service and dismantled in 1938.

When first delivered in 1909, Type F car 214 represented the height of modernity. It certainly was an improvement on the open toppers that had preceded it. Note the MSC number on the lower bulkhead panel. *D. Jones Collection*

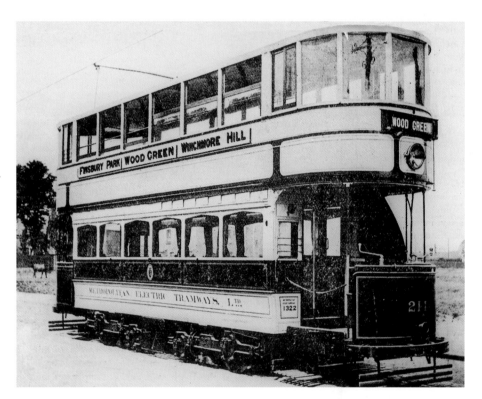

Type G. Cars 217–236, 317

Built in 1909 by Brush of Loughborough, these twenty open top tramcars could accommodate 32 people in the lower deck and 42 on the upper one. They received the standard MET Mountain & Gibson bogies with 40hp motors. Plough carriers were subsequently attached to the trucks. Rheostatic, hand wheel and magnetic track brakes were fitted as standard.

Modernisation took the usual form. All-enclosed top covers were added in 1928–1930 and transverse seats were installed in the lower saloon. Seats on both decks were then reupholstered in grey/green Moquettino fabric. Driver's windscreens were fitted in 1931 and cars 217–236 were renumbered in the LT 2262–2281 series.

Car 317 was constructed by the staff at Hendon Works in 1921. It was allocated to Type G and its history after it went out on the road is similar to other members of the group. It became London Transport car 2261 and was scrapped in December 1938.

Type G car 225 is depicted surrounded by much transport interest in the form of an LT type General bus working from Leyton Garage, an LCC E/1 car on service 81 and an E/3 on Kingsway Subway service 35. Dark blue and white OAKEYS adverts adorn both trams.

Below left Upholstered seats, double bulkhead doors, straps for standing passengers and a centrally placed bell cord can all be noted in this view of the lower saloon of a Type G car. A fare chart was usually posted on the left hand bulkhead window.

Below Type G car 231, metamorphosed into LT car 2276, stands at North Finchley tram station shortly before the conversion of route 21 to trolleybus routes 521/621. The scrapping of such robust vehicles was greeted with dismay by those tramway students who claimed that these cars could have had their active lives prolonged south of the River Thames.

The Type G trams gained a reputation for being robust, reliable vehicles and they deserved better than to be sent for scrap in 1938. Some tramway students of the era maintained that many MET G and H type cars gave as good a ride as the replacing trolleybuses and that they were in better condition than many former LCC vehicles, which survived in South London into the early postwar years.

Type H. Cars 237–316, 2(II), 12(II), 22(II), 31(II), 46(II) and 82(II)

These trams constituted the largest single class in the MET fleet. They were substantially built vehicles, supplied in 1909–1912 by Brush of Loughborough. Two General Electric 40hp motors were supplied as standard, although these were later replaced by higher rated equipment in the modernisation programme. Cars 237–241 possessed Mountain & Gibson Type 3L maximum traction trucks, whilst cars 242–316 used Brush trucks of a very similar design.

Longitudinal seats for 32 in the lower saloon were replaced in the late 1920s by two-and-one upholstered transverse seats for 12, plus four new longitudinal seats for 16 passengers. On the fully enclosed upper deck there was space for 46 people on wooden seats. Only a few of Type H would later receive upholstered seating in the upper saloon. There was always some doubt that upper saloon passengers needed cushioned seats, and there were concerns about keeping the seats clean in the smoky atmosphere that often prevailed on the top deck.

Cars 2, 12, 22, 31, 46 and 82 were second series vehicles built at Hendon Works in 1925–26. They took the fleet numbers of scrapped Type A and B trams. In bodywork and electrical equipment these five vehicles resembled standard Type H cars. They were fitted experimentally with heaters to gauge passenger reaction during cold winter weather.

After incorporation into the London Transport fleet cars 237–314 were renumbered 2169–2246; cars 315 and 316 became 2254 and 2247 respectively. The numbers 2248–2253 were allocated to the second series. The last member of Type H perished early in 1939.

This official Brush Company photograph, taken at the works in Loughborough, shows one of the Type H vehicles before delivery to the MET. It has yet to be equipped with lifeguards, but is otherwise in pristine condition. On the stair stringer the notice reads PASSENGERS ENTERING OR LEAVING THE CAR WHILE IN MOTION DO SO AT THEIR OWN RISK. There is also a reminder printed above the nearside bulkhead window that no dogs are allowed on the car.

Type H car 258 is shown at Waltham Cross, with the cross itself in the background.

Works Cars

These were essential to the efficient operation of the network and they were numbered in the series 01–014. They attracted little attention from the general public and merited few column inches in the technical press. Hence, the following list represents the state of research at the present time. Some details concerning the works fleet are conjectural and cannot be confirmed directly by photographic evidence.

Cars 01, 02, 03 and 04(II) were water cars used in the early years to keep the dust down during the summer months. Road surfaces subject to horse drawn traffic needed regular cleaning and these service vehicles with their large water tanks could do the job. They were also called upon to lubricate sharp curves. Car 4(II) was former SOUTHMET car 47 and was also used as a water car and a rail grinder.

Car 02(II) was designated as a wheel carrier. It would deliver wheel sets, axles and other heavy items to depots. For this purpose it was equipped with block and tackle lifting gear. Car 04 was a stores van, which also functioned as a delivery vehicle. Lighter items, such as ticket stocks and other goods that could be carried or manhandled, were ferried about by Car 04. Sandbags were transported by car 05, which was a particularly interesting vehicle in that the car body was mounted on a six wheel Barber radial truck. This was an experimental design and it was replaced after two years use by a conventional single truck.

Two track breaking vehicles, cars 03(II) and 03(III), were employed on permanent way maintenance. As their name suggests, they possessed heavy pile driving and drilling equipment to open up the roadway prior to rails being replaced. Figures issued for 1928–29 indicated that the MET had a total of 53.46 route miles (86km), most of which was situated on the public highway; added to this were 3.78 miles (6km) of sidings and depot trackage.

Cars 06, 07, 07(II), 08, 09, 010, 010(II), 011, 012, 013 and 014 functioned as general purpose breakdown cars. All were retired passenger vehicles that had had their lower deck seating stripped out to accommodate tools and maintenance materials. Finally, car 09(II) was known as a salt car. Its purpose was to help clear lines in winter weather. Although trucks and motors were robustly built, impacted snow lying between the rails could easily damage car lifeguards, thus rendering any tram unusable in passenger service.

Non railbound works vehicles included a number of horse drawn tower wagons needed for the erection and maintenance of the overhead wiring. As the internal combustion engine became more reliable, inspection towers and ladders were mounted on lorry chassis. At one stage in the 1920s the MET possessed five motor tower wagons that were housed at depots around the system. They had to be ready to respond to any emergency calls. Overhead lines were energised at 550 volts direct current, so any potential danger to tram crews and the general public had to be dealt with promptly.

Two Foden 5-ton steam wagons, registered M 8628 and NK 1671, were used for heavy duty work involving the transport of rail sections. Several motor lorries and vans were also on the company's books. In later years these had effectively taken over most of the delivery tasks formerly allocated to the works tram fleet. The MET also supplied its chief officers with private motor cars, so that they could arrive at offices and depots in style. It was felt that they had sufficient status not to commute to work by tram!

Water car 02 is about to leave the confines of Hendon Depot. The driver's left hand moves the controller handle to apply power to the motors, whilst his other hand slackens the handbrake. *LT Museum*

Below Car 05 of the works fleet leaves observers in no doubt as to its departmental function. It carried bags of dried sand from a store in Wood Green Depot out to the other depots in the MET empire. *D. Jones Collection*

Car 318, Bluebell

Bluebell has been described as London's first modern tramcar. It might be more accurate to place this vehicle in a transitional category between the standard London bogie car and the modern Felthams, which were to appear at the end of the 1920s. Outwardly, as the photograph on the left shows, Bluebell still looked quite traditional. This impression was enhanced by the use of tried and tested LCC type maximum traction trucks – there was nothing revolutionary in the running gear. Indeed, it was originally intended to fit conduit plough equipment to one of the trucks, so that car 318 would not be barred from operating into central London.

A break with accepted tramway practice came with the installation of two sets of doors on each side of the car. These formed part of the passenger flow design, whereby people entered and left by different doorways. This meant that both of the tram's internal staircases could be used independently of the direction of the car. On a standard double decker passengers could not board or alight from the motorman's platform; they were restricted to one staircase at the conductor's end of the car.

Bluebell's driver had a rather cramped compartment to himself. Because of police regulations no windscreen was fitted, although each vestibule was part glazed with an early non-inflammable transparent plastic material. Upholstered seats were provided for 27 in the lower saloon and for 44 on the upper deck.

Other important details were covered in an article that appeared in the *TOT Staff Magazine* for February 1927. Some of the more technical aspects of Bluebell are described:

Altogether, the new car is four and a half tons lighter than those of the old type having the same seating capacity. No (internal) doors or framework are necessary on the top deck, as the car is of the vestibule type and all draughts are consequently eliminated.

Powerful motors are installed which are geared to driving wheels fitted with roller bearings. Air brakes control the stops, which are further facilitated by a device that blows sand directly under the wheels . . . A master controller is fitted. Beside the numerous levers, handles and wheels manipulated by the motorman, there is another arrangement by which he controls the doors of the front platform, so that passengers can leave by that end.

As a pioneer of the new order, Bluebell No.318 forges ahead. Her high powered motors mean increased speed, air brakes and sand control mean safety; even a front platform exit must affect the system of fare collecting. The skilled motorman, his hands on the controls, his eyes along the track, is making progress far more quickly than he dreams.

Unfortunately, the safety features of the new car failed at the first real test. On 17th June 1927, Bluebell collided with a Scammell heavy lorry on Barnet Hill by the Station Approach. Motorman Maurice Kent's driving cab became a death trap. Suspicion fell on lack of sufficient air braking, but nothing was proven at the subsequent accident enquiry. Severely damaged at one end, car 318 was withdrawn from service and rebuilt. In this form it re-entered service in the spring of 1928. As can be seen from the photograph opposite, the most striking element of the reconstruction was added in the following year, when a domed aluminium roof was fitted. Bluebell survived into London Transport days to be renumbered 2255. Unfortunately, its unique design status counted for very little with the new owners and the vehicle was cut up in October 1937.

Metropolitan Police regulations dictated that no windscreen should 'interfere' with the motorman's view of the road ahead – at least this way he had no need of windscreen wipers, when it was tipping down! This view is dated February 1927. *LT Museum*

Car 318, Bluebell, incorporated modern ideas into what was essentially a traditional design. Note the separate entrance and exit, plus the driver's compartment, clear of the staircase. *LT Museum*

Car 318 in its rebuilt form displays several changes in livery details as well as the pronounced domed roof. This feature, and the pale blue paint scheme, made the car instantly identifiable. *LT Museum*

Car 319, Poppy

Poppy was built at the Chiswick Works of the London General Omnibus Company and she entered revenue service in April 1927. Obvious comparisons were made with car 318 and not only in the distinctive liveries of both trams. The red colour of Poppy contrasted with the light blue of Bluebell. The fact that car 319 was painted LGOC red and that it resembled two NS-type buses shoved together, caused raised eyebrows in the tramway fraternity. From some angles the car looked quite sleek – avant-garde even – but the aesthetics worsened as the car was viewed in broadside. This revealed a distinctly ugly arrangement of differing window sizes. The extended canopies above each driving platform did not seem in proportion to the rest of the car. In short, unlike sister car 318, Poppy never caught the imagination of the travelling public, nor did the experimental vehicle appeal to the management of the Combine tramways. Put bluntly, she was a hybrid. On the positive side, emphasis was placed on passenger comfort above seating capacity. Hence, Poppy could only accommodate 28 in the lower saloon and 36 on the top deck.

After Bluebell was involved in the fatal Barnet Hill accident, car 319 was temporarily withdrawn from service. Conventional magnetic track brakes were fitted, but Poppy's days on the MET were over. In November 1927 she was renumbered 350 in the London United fleet after her transfer to West London. She survived long enough to become London Transport car 2317 and was sent for scrap in November 1935.

According to legend, when the MET staff first laid eyes on car 319 it confirmed their prejudices about 'those bus people at Chiswick'. They had produced a monstrosity of a tram and they couldn't even get the fleet number right! In modern parlance the Chiswick coachbuilders had put together two bus fronts to create a 'stretch limo' on rails. Needless to say, this experiment was not repeated.
LT Museum

Readers must make their own judgement whether this end view is any more stylish than the broadside perspective. At least the Metropolitan Police Commissioner would be pleased – the driver had nothing at all to obstruct his forward vision. There were drain holes in the floor to let rainwater out! *LT Museum*

As an addendum to the Bluebell and Poppy saga, C.J. Spencer expressed his views in the 9th June 1932 issue of *Tramway & Railway World*:

The time did arrive when I was authorised to build a tramcar . . . and by way of a spur to action, my colleague of the omnibus company was asked to build one – a kind of tram-omnibus. In 1927 these two tramcars were put into service, and were christened by the staff "Bluebell" and "Poppy".

I need hardly say anything about these two tramcars, as they had a good deal of publicity at the time and represented the first serious attempt which we in London made to break away from tradition and devise something quite new in the British tramway world.

Paired Cars 151 & 164, 56 & 82

General Manager C.J. Spencer and his deputy, A.V. Mason, put their heads together to convince the powers that be to let them experiment. Two trams coupled together to form a short train emerged from Hendon Works in 1921. Type C/2 bogie cars 151 and 164 were linked by new control equipment and it was originally intended to use them on the western side of the MET system. Then the quibbling began. Nobody could agree on where they would be allowed to run. To cut a long story short, Metropolitan Police concerns finally dictated that the vehicles' operation be limited to an itinerary from the Hampstead boundary spur at Childs Hill to Tally Ho Corner, North Finchley.

Electrical problems surfaced with the controllers. Engineers from the English Electric Company had to be called in to sort the matter out. During 1926 the set was employed in peak hour service and performed creditably. Although the two trams could be fed by a single trolley pole, in practice when out on the road, both trolleys were used. The experiment was terminated at the end of 1926 and cars 151 and 164 resumed their respective independent existences. Some tramwaymen thought the whole thing was jinxed from the start and that precious time and money had been wasted. The abandonment of the LCC trailers in 1923–24 was cited as proof that tramway vehicles coupled together had no place on British streets. Linked units were considered slow, with a penchant to hold up the rest of the traffic.

Bearing in mind the lukewarm response to the earlier coupled set, it is interesting to speculate what the motives were in having another go, this time with cars 56, converted to single-deck and 82. From an economic standpoint there was always the possibility of saving on staff costs by employing three men per set – one motorman and two conductors. However, the Metropolitan Police, who had a big say in what was permitted to operate on the roads of the capital, tended to regard any tramcar as an obstruction to traffic. Therefore, by the same logic, two trams linked together represented twice the obstruction, with the possibility that any mechanical failure could result in a major problem in shifting the vehicles from the public carriageway.

Car 56 was stripped of its top deck fittings and was given an all-round vestibule at the far end away from its sister car 82. This combination of a double decker and a single decker may have looked odd to the general public. Several outings were undertaken during the latter half of 1927, but police objections to the efficiency of air brakes in London tramway operation curtailed the experiment. Eventually, Messrs Spencer and Mason lost interest and the whole thing fizzled out. Car 56 was scrapped in 1929; Type H car 82 lost its status as one half of a twin set and was returned to public service as a conventional vehicle.

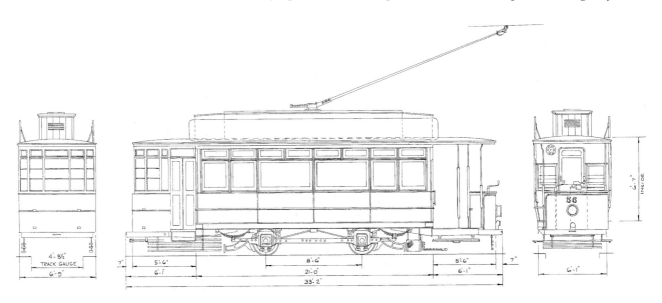

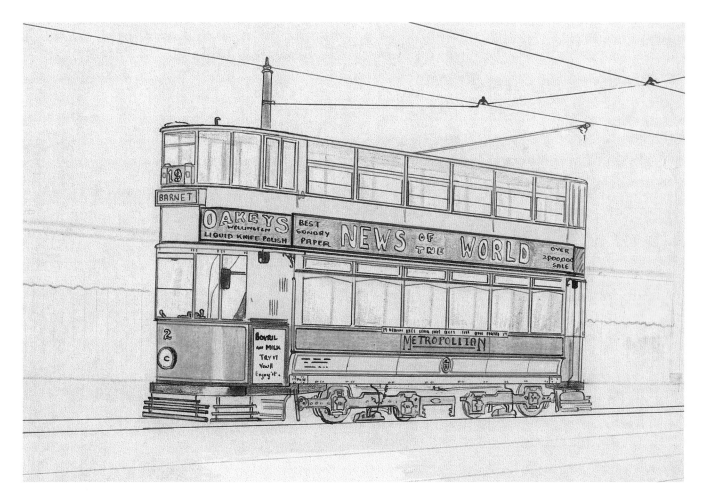

Tramcar Liveries

With the obvious exception of car 318, Bluebell, the main colour of the MET fleet was red. Members of the Middlesex County Council Light Railways Committee specified 'vermilion picked out creamy white' – in plain terms this meant a red and white livery. The red colour was applied over a white or pink undercoat. At first, trucks, fenders and controllers were black. Later on, trucks, lifeguards and trolley masts on open top cars were painted red oxide. For a complete impression of the original MET paint scheme, reference should be made to the illustration of car 193 on page 4.

From 1929 onwards the livery was simplified and much of the ornate lining on the waist and rocker panels was omitted. Car 331, illustrated on page 115, shows the last form of the Metropolitan Electric Tramways livery.

Metropolitan Stage Carriage Licences

Trams, buses and cabs operating in London had to be licensed by the Commissioner of the Metropolitan Police. In practice every vehicle in the MET fleet that ran in public service was obliged to have a Metropolitan Stage Carriage Licence Plate (MSC Plate). An annual inspection of each vehicle to verify its roadworthiness was part of the procedure in renewing the licence. The MSC Plate was generally displayed at one end of the car on the exterior lower panel of the bulkhead.

Don Thompson lived in Lordship Lane and was able to observe tramway operation at first hand. He prepared a series of coloured drawings in 1940. In the dark days of the Second World War they served to remind him of the happier days of his childhood. The originals are now in the possession of the London County Council Tramways Trust.

8. WAR AND PEACE

The outbreak of the First World War on 4th August 1914 and the mobilisation of the military had an immediate effect on the nation's transport systems. Horses were requisitioned; many of the beasts that were herded into the grounds of Alexandra Palace successfully made the swap from baker's van to gun carriage. Motor vehicles also had a role to play in transporting the British Expeditionary Force to the battlefields in Flanders. No fewer than 300 buses and 330 drivers from the London area were commandeered by the army to make the trip to the Western Front. At this time it was confidently expected that hostilities would cease in December and the war would be over by Christmas. Unfortunately, this scenario was a false one and some of those MET employees who volunteered to join the colours did not live to see the end of the conflict. The names of the fallen were later inscribed on war memorials at each depot.

It might be assumed that, since joining the ranks of the Combine, the prospects of the MET were particularly rosy. This outlook seemed to be confirmed by an increase in passengers due to wartime conditions. Restrictions on bus travel, the expansion of munitions factories plus growing numbers of men and women engaged on war work – all these factors combined to fill the trams to capacity. However, appearances can be deceptive and it became increasingly difficult for the Company to maintain track and rolling stock to an acceptable standard. Shortages of steel and other raw materials had a serious impact on the network. In the seven years from 1907 to 1914 working costs had more than doubled. This left precious little cash to cover fleet renewals. Arguably, war or no war, the Company was in a parlous state. Already, unofficial discussions were taking place with the relevant authorities to alleviate the Company's indebtedness to Middlesex County Council. Clearly, a way had to be found to gain further capital investment in the tramways system.

The tube and bus shareholders, who claimed that the Combine had been sold a pup with its tramway investments, seemed to have their fears confirmed when in 1917 an official receiver had to be called in to manage the LUT's affairs. This was particularly inconvenient for the MET, because a single track connection between the two systems at Acton had been constructed in July 1915. A pressing reason for the link was that the LUT repair works at Chiswick had been requisitioned for the munitions industry, thus forcing the LUT to consider using Hendon Works as an alternative. Although there was much doubt as to whether the LUT could actually pay for the services provided, the cash strapped MET board could hardly deny the request, bearing in mind the pressing needs of the war effort.

A view within the confines of the depot yard at Stonebridge Park. Note the wealth of small details, such as the rather grimy looking tap on the right hand wall, above which is a notice marked DRINKING WATER! The motorman of car 10, his driving goggles wrapped round his cap, is probably above the age of conscription to serve on the Western Front. The conductress seems happy to smile for the photographer. After they both get out on to the road, she would have her work cut out to collect all the fares of the munitions and factory workers, who regularly used the Harrow Road line. *D. Jones Collection*

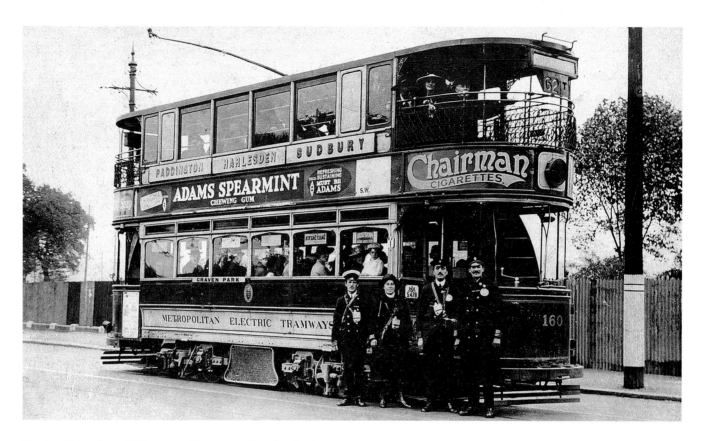

The headlight of car 160 is covered in order to conform to wartime blackout restrictions. The appearance of a lone conductress is further evidence of the changed working conditions imposed during the 1914–1918 conflict. All the staff pictured here are attached to Stonebridge Park Depot.

Further bad news emanated from the MET, as it became clear that continued participation in the recently established joint services to central London could not be guaranteed. The official excuse for the termination of through running was that the Company lacked sufficient conduit equipped vehicles to maintain schedules. On 1st May 1916 service 51 succumbed, followed on 26th February 1917 by the demise of service 19. In both cases the LCC and the MET tried to make up the deficit by running extra cars on their respective sides of the county boundary. On 2nd May 1917 service 21 was split at Finsbury Park. Through trams continued to work on services 9, 27, 29, 59 and 79. This must have been particularly welcomed by war workers travelling out to the factories north of Ponders End, where employees now laboured on shifts through a 7-day week. Industrial demands were so acute that the MET was forced to adopt the most unBritish practice of offering workmen's fares on Sundays!

On the western side of the system factories making everything from small arms to complete aircraft bodies had been established in the Park Royal and Edgware Road areas. Heavy passenger loadings and a shortage of drivers encouraged A.H. Pott, MET Chief Engineer and General Manager (1902–1918), to ask the Board of Trade to sanction trailer operation. Although this method of tramway working was universally employed abroad, it was not popular in the UK. One of the chief objectors to trailer cars was the Commissioner of the Metropolitan Police. The sticking points concerned braking arrangements, passenger safety and disruption to other road users at termini, where the whole tractor and trailer set had to be reversed. Unfortunately, turning loops, which could have assisted trailer operation, were notable by their absence on British tramways.

The trailer proposal eventually died the death. In order to maintain the status quo, the Company had to compromise in other ways. Tram services not deemed vital to the war effort were cut. The recruitment of conductresses was partly successful in filling vacancies left by platform staff, who had joined the military; however, approval for motorwomen was blocked by the Metropolitan Police. Female tram drivers never did make an appearance in London.

The military authorities also had their eyes on several of the Company's tramcars, as well as on male tramway employees, as potential recruits. The trams were going to be borrowed for the duration to serve as searchlight cars in order to combat the increasing menace of attacks by enemy airships. One car was regularly positioned at the end of the track by Barnet Church. During the evening of 1st October 1916 and into the early hours of the next day, a prolonged Zeppelin raid took place over North London. One of the giant airships, L31, was illuminated by the beam of the Barnet searchlight tram. This enabled Wulstan Joseph Tempest, a 2nd Lieutenant in the 39th Home Defence Squadron, based at Hornchurch, to fire on the enemy from his fighter aircraft, thus igniting the hydrogen gas in the airship. Then, to the cheers of the assembled multitude outside Barnet Church, the Zeppelin burst into flames and went down with all hands; every member of the German crew was incinerated.

Whether any of the MET Type A uncanopied bogie cars were used as searchlight trams is a matter of debate. It seems more likely that a number of similar looking LUT Type X vehicles were requisitioned. The irony was that, although the London United was practically bankrupt, it still had trams to spare. The cars from West Middlesex were then shunted over into MET territory in the early months of 1916. Each tram was painted War Office green, with the searchlight mounted on the top deck. Crew members from the Royal Engineers were housed in the lower saloon, which was converted into a mess room. This ingenious use of tramcars proved to be a temporary measure and the last of the six vehicles adapted for the defence of the realm was returned to civilian life in March 1917.

Lighting restrictions on the trams had been in force since 1914. Although the imposition of blackout regulations in the First World War was not as comprehensive as it was in the 1939–1945 conflict, the authorities were still worried about excessive illumination and the possibility of trams using the Hertford Road causing sparking from the overhead wires. In short, fears were expressed that an enemy navigator might get a fix on a vital munitions factory in the Enfield Highway area. Eventually, tram headlamps were covered with black paint, leaving only two small side lights fixed on either side of the top deck above the motorman. The problem of flashes resulting from the interaction of trolley wheel and overhead wire, especially in icy or wet weather, was never satisfactorily solved.

Towards the end of the war, joint service 19 reappeared on 2nd September 1918. Progress was then interrupted for almost two years, until service 51 returned on 7th July 1920, to be followed by service 21 on 27th October. Lack of conduit fitted MET cars was again cited as the reason for the delay in restoring the through routes. In fact, the precise nature of the MET's troubles lay in unsuitability of many of its early bogie cars for conduit plough gear. When a number of single truck cars of Type D were adapted to run over the LCC lines there was a predictable outcry from the LCC, but the situation in the immediate postwar months regarding replacement vehicles must have been so dire, both nationally and locally, that the LCC was forced to acquiesce. Open top Type D trams worked service 51, continuing until 1931.

Through services have recommenced and Car 297, on route 29 to Tottenham Court Road, is seen here at Wood Green. The junction in the foreground was originally the only 'grand union' on the system. The east to west track linking Station Road and Lordship Lane was severed sometime near the end of the First World War. *D. Jones Collection*

The operational philosophy of the three Combine tramways in the period 1919–1921 can be summed up in the phrase 'make do and mend'. An increasingly important role in the rehabilitation of rolling stock and services would be played by Christopher John Spencer, who succeeded A.H. Pott as General Manager in October 1918. Although no more new lines were constructed, it was under Spencer's stewardship

that the downward slide appeared to have been halted. In fact, in 1920, before the real impact of intensive bus competition was felt, a record 126,867,379 passengers were carried by the MET. This improving state of affairs was confirmed in the following year, when traffic receipts topped the million pound mark for the first time.

However, in spite of the apparent success in attracting customers, there was still much work to do in order to make the system profitable for the long term. Important shortcomings still needed to be solved. The situation at transfer points such as Finsbury Park could be described as chaotic in peak hours. Hordes of passengers emerging from the tube station would mill around in the busy roadway. The construction of loading islands for the trams and extra approach tracks would have gone some way to alleviate the congestion, but funds were not forthcoming. Nor could the local authorities and the two tramway operators agree on where the rails should go and, more crucially, who should foot the bill. Then the Metropolitan Police stepped in to quash an imaginative plan for a siding to be laid on private right of way in the park grounds. In short, in time honoured British parochial fashion, the mess was left to sort itself out.

Critics used the traffic problems generated in the area as a stick to beat the tramways. Already in the 1915 *Annual Report of the London Traffic Branch of the Board of Trade* a new linguistic term, dubbed the Traffic Unit, which represented a coefficient of obstruction, had been invented. This official gobbledegook was meant to categorise vehicles in terms of their size, speed and flexibility on the highway. Inevitably, the electric tram with a score of 9 units came out top, way ahead of its rivals – the motorbus (4 units) and the motor cab (1 unit). One would have thought that with a world war raging the motoring lobby would have had better things to do with its time than putting the knife into the tramcar. After all, the capital's tramways were doing a splendid job in transporting large numbers of workers to munitions factories. However, from the end of the war onwards, protests from the 'scrap the trams in London' brigade became more vocal. To many of the well off in society the reality of an Edwardian tramcar lumbering along in the middle of the street did not match the image of the Roaring Twenties and Jazz Age. The Bright Young Things were more attuned to private motoring and its promise of speed and freedom.

In contrast to events happening elsewhere, a welcome boost to the Company came on 2nd June 1920, when through running commenced at Stamford Hill. This time, unlike the situation with route 51 and the open toppers, the Company found the wherewithal to fit bogie cars with plough carriers. LCC vehicles operated exclusively on service 49 from Liverpool Street, which was extended over MET tracks to terminate at Edmonton Town Hall. The joint service mileage agreement was balanced out by the LCC withdrawing their vehicles from services 59 and 79.

An added tramway connection in the area came in the shape of a new LCC line. Before the outbreak of the 1914–1918 war the County Council had promoted a scheme for a route from Stamford Hill to a junction with MET rails in Seven Sisters Road. Work eventually started on the new line along Amhurst Park in August 1923. It was equipped for overhead trolley operation and opened for service 53 cars on 31st March 1924.

The apparent expansionist policies of the LCC were not mirrored north of the county boundary, where pressures on the MET continued to mount. In his 1921 Annual Report the Middlesex County Surveyor painted a sombre picture of the state of the county's tramways. He was concerned with the poor condition of the permanent way and the surrounding road structure. He cited the increase in motor traffic as a major contributory factor in the deterioration of the tram track. He was also of the opinion that remedial work would have to wait until funds were available. He noted that any reconstruction programme was 'likely to be a slow process'.

The financial health of the undertaking was becoming weaker. In 1920 a proposal from the MET to charge a minimum fare of 2d ran into opposition and there were howls of protest when the Company asked permission to scrap workmen's fares. These concessions to the working population were enshrined in Parliamentary statute and would remain part of the fare structure of London's tramways until 1st October 1950, some twenty-one months before the end of the system in July 1952.

Added to the loss of fare revenue was the spectacle of competition from the numerous pirate buses that had sprung up from the summer of 1922. Ironically, although the Armistice had concluded hostilities on the battlefield, war was about to break out on the streets of the capital. A multitude of brightly coloured vehicles were now undercutting the fares of other established public transport operators. Licensed by the Metropolitan Police, the names spanned the alphabet from the A1 Omnibus Company run by a Mr Collins to the X-Service operated by L.S. Punnett. Researchers have recorded a total of no fewer than 366 different companies in the heyday of the pirate. Of course, the term 'pirate' appealed neither to omnibus owners nor to supporters of private enterprise. Since they were not associated with the Combine and the LGOC, the new boys chose to style themselves 'independent' bus operators.

These independents soon fastened on to MET trunk routes. Irresponsible driving led to many accidents, as buses sought to use their speed to cut in front of trams in order to steal passengers. Competing crews sometimes came to blows and the police had to be summoned to sort out the ensuing fracas. Thus, rampant chaos emerged out of the order imposed on London's traffic by war conditions. Clearly, if this situation continued, the MET would risk defaulting on rent and loan repayments. A part solution to the problem, when it came in 1924, would serve to prolong the life of all metropolitan tramway operators.

This view of Church Road, Willesden conveys the atmosphere of the early postwar years. The MET fleet has been stretched to the limit and track and infrastructure now need urgent attention. Open top cars 8 and 46, seen here, look distinctly antiquated.

This motorman would be wearing a
dark blue serge suit with red piping.
The overcoat and leather gauntlets
were necessary to cope with the
rigours of life on an open fronted
tramcar. The cap badge is the familiar
Combine 'bar and circle' device in
dark blue with silver lettering.
D. Jones Collection

9. A Tramwayman's Life

Tram crews in horse-car days were a tough lot. Drivers and conductors had to be out in all weathers and they could expect to work an average of ten hours a day, six days a week. However, there were no set contracts to prevent employers making extra demands if, in their opinion, traffic conditions warranted a longer working day. Furthermore, anyone questioning the status quo or caught trying to organise a trade union risked instant dismissal. There were always two or three people waiting in the wings to fill the shoes of any unfortunate who lost his job. Rates of pay varied across the capital. A conductor might earn twenty-seven shillings (£1.35) for a 60 hour week; his driver could expect to receive around thirty shillings (£1.50) for his labours.

Social events, like the annual company sports day, were a welcome relief to the workaday world of tram driving and conducting. It was an occasion to bring the family. Transport, courtesy of the MET, was provided free of charge. Everyone had to look smart in their 'Sunday best'. Entertainment and refreshments were laid on for the journey. *LCC Tramways Trust Collection*

A wonderful evocation of life at the end of the Victorian era was published in the *TOT Staff Magazine* for December 1927. Inspector W.T. Davies of the MET, who retired at the age of seventy, recalled the old days in this edited version of his memoirs:

It was in September 1879 – I was taken on as a conductor by the old North Metropolitan Tramways Company . . . By way of breaking in, I did two journeys with a service man on the Moorgate Street and Manor House line, and then started in earnest the very next day on the Moorgate Street and Abney Park service. This line ended at the Weavers Arms, a few years later it was extended to Stamford Hill. The hours were pretty long and the pay wasn't exactly big, and there were no regular meal times – had to have the grub on the car in the slack hours, the cars then being run into the sheds for a short time. When a second car came in the first one went out again, and so on, so a fellow sometimes didn't get time for more than a bite. This state of things was altered when Mr Adamson came as manager. He arranged regular meal times by means of reliefs.

There were no uniforms for tramwaymen in those days, or for busmen, either, for that matter. The tramway drivers and conductors had a cap given to them by the company and that was all.

Fares? Oh, yes, I remember the early fares all right. To begin with, there weren't any penny fares. Fourpence was charged for the through journey, with intermediate fares of twopence and threepence. Twopence was the minimum. And there were no tickets, but when you had an excess fare you gave the passenger a slip ticket as a sort of receipt . . .

One of my most vivid recollections is the terrible winter of 1881. In January we had a regular blizzard, with the heaviest fall of snow I've ever seen . . . We tramwaymen went out with shovels and cleared the tramway track by throwing the snow to the side, so that we made a sort of pathway between great banks of snow. Then we got a service started, with six horses to each car, the horses being driven by a service driver on the platform and two postilions. Of course, the only bit of the road along which a passage could be made was the tramway track. Other vehicles ran in front when the cars started from the Weavers Arms and we had to follow them, at whatever speed they went, all the way to Dalston, where there was the first cross service of trams, before the ordinary traffic could get out of the trench.

In 1888, I was transferred to the Manor House terminus as Timekeeper. The North Metropolitan trams ran from the Manor House to the City by way of Green Lanes and the New North Road. The other lines at the Manor House belonged to the old North London Company, which owned the steam trams. One line went from Finsbury Park to Ponders End, the other from Finsbury Park to The Nightingale at Wood Green. The cars were pulled by locomotives, which used to break down pretty frequently. And when one broke down, there it stayed until the next loco and car came up and shoved it along behind . . .

I finished up with the MET last August. Seventy-one I am now . . . And if you ask me what is the best change I have seen since I started as a tramwayman, I should say the change in conditions of employment. Better hours, better pay, uniforms and a few other things, not forgetting a week's holiday. Lord! It'd make anybody smile in the old days to think of a tramwayman having a week's holiday . . .

The North Metropolitan ranked as one of the more progressive employers. The management set up a provident society for the welfare of the workers. Membership was not compulsory, but a contribution of sixpence (2.5p) a week ensured at least some benefits should a tramway man suffer illness or injury. In deserving cases an award of two shillings and sixpence (12.5p) sick pay could be granted. In an age when mortality rates among young men were higher, the death of the breadwinner in the household could have dire financial consequences. In these circumstances the North Metropolitan provident fund could pay a grant of up to £15. Additional income for tram crews was dependent on the generosity of the travelling public. Over the Christmas period tramway companies usually allowed a collecting box to be placed in each tramcar. Drivers and conductors were under strict instructions not to solicit contributions.

Working conditions remained rather Spartan even under the new British Electric Traction Company regime. Those further up the BET company tree might expect an invitation to the annual staff dinner. One such took place at the Criterion Restaurant on Friday, 25th July 1902. The Managing Director, Emile Garcke, spoke to the assembled group of 240 senior employees. After this pep talk the *BET Gazette* noted: *Mr. Garcke's spirit and energy imbued the whole organisation . . . An excellent selection of music was played during dinner, and the solidity of the speech programme was relieved by songs, recitations and musical sketches.* Almost certainly, some of those enjoying themselves at the Criterion Restaurant had a hand in the BET's decision two years previously that 'wanted the Annual Supper for workers to be discontinued' (I quote). Although Ebenezer Scrooge and Jacob Marley were not officially listed as BET directors, their penny pinching philosophy underpinned the thinking that the meagre distribution of Christmas box money would suffice for platform staff.

This meanness of spirit by the upper echelons of the BET would not be forgotten, but, on the other hand, the organisation could also show a more humane face to employees. The British Electrical Friendly Society was established to provide sick pay and death grants. The 1902–1903 report of the Society, one of whose committee members was Emile Garcke, listed 47 members at Edmonton Depot, 33 at Manor House and 52 at Wood Green. These people had been admitted to the BEFS on 27th January 1903. However, out of a total MET workforce of 324, this still meant that some 192 individuals probably had no cover whatsoever for a rainy day.

On 1st January 1905 the BET launched an enhanced welfare scheme, which included provision for a pension fund to be set up under the auspices of the British Electrical Provident Fund. In addition to the sixpence a week subscription to the sick pay fund, each employee had the choice of a weekly 4d, 6d or 9d contribution to the pension fund. Benefits quoted in the *BET Gazette* could amount to a sum of twenty shillings a week sick pay, with a pension at the age of 60 of six shillings a week.

Basic training for crews consisted of road experience. Apprentice conductors would be sent out to learn the ropes with another conductor, who had already mastered the route and the intricacies of the fare stages. On the publication of the recommendations of the inspecting officer in the Highgate accident report, we are told that the hapless Driver Cone's training 'consisted of eleven lessons of about one hour each in the School . . . and twelve lessons (amounting to 98 hours) on the road. He then had three days' practice on the Archway route with another motorman (including one day's instruction in the use of the magnetic brake).' After this, Driver Cone and all his fellow rookie motormen were on their own.

Training periods were lengthened after the report, and precedence was given to experienced drivers on routes with potentially difficult conditions, such as sharp bends and steep gradients. The MET also later consulted officials of the Southmet to ask what advice they gave to their drivers in order to cope with the 1 in 9.5 (10.5%) gradient on Anerley Hill.

Concern was also felt at the high number of tram drivers succumbing to illness during the winter months. Obviously, an exposed driving position at the front of the car required suitable protective clothing for each motorman. In the hope that claims on the sick fund would be reduced, the BET Friendly Society arranged to have heavy duty gloves or gauntlets supplied at a cost of half a crown (12.5p) a pair. It was still expected that each motorman would come dressed in his own overcoat, but at least his fingers could be kept warm at the Friendly Society's expense. No provision was made for canteen or recreational facilities for staff; lunch breaks were unknown. Sustaining hot meals or drinks had to be consumed whilst on the road. The normal procedure was that a relative of the conductor or motorman would meet the tram at some convenient point in its journey to hand over the food.

Although the addition of a recreation room at each depot lay in the future, the BET did encourage its staff to remain fit by joining in various sporting activities. The Metropolitan Electric Tramways Athletic Club was divided into two sections – the officials and the men, commonly known as the 'salaries' and the 'wages'! On Wednesday, 12th July 1905, a cricket match was arranged with teams representing MET Staff and MET Officials. The Staff batted first and managed 40 runs; it was reported in the *Gazette* that Motorman Wilkinson was top scorer with 10 runs. When the Officials took the field they had no difficulty in amassing a winning total of 72 runs. Stumps were drawn at six o'clock and 'an excellent tea' was provided by the Company and this proved 'a good finish to a most enjoyable game'.

A number of fixtures were arranged for the MET football and cricket teams, and interest amongst the staff remained high throughout the years of BET ownership. Indeed, the sporting prowess of the Metropolitan Electric was such that it could take on a representative team drawn from the rest of the BET fold. Early in 1906 at Edmonton the North London boys had triumphed by four goals to one. The BET were anxious to avenge this defeat and a return match was organised on Wednesday, 28th March. The BET team came prepared and were two goals up in the first five minutes. Such was the superiority of the BET players that, as the *BET Gazette* noted: 'it was on few occasions that the MET forwards crossed the halfway line'. The rout was completed, as the BET netted three further times without reply from the MET.

On and off the sports field the Metropolitan Electric Tramways Company owed much to its loyal and dedicated employees. Everyone from the platform and depot staff to the clerks in the Manor House office had a part to play. The *BET Gazette* for 23rd January 1907 lists 471 members of the Traffic Department and 234 members of the Engineering Department. We are told there were 36 inspectors, timekeepers and regulators, who supervised 395 motormen and conductors. Other occupations attached to the Traffic Department included 17 trolley and point boys, 7 female clerks and typists, 1 coachman and 1 caretaker. The seven female clerks were all unmarried ladies. If a female employee got married, she would be asked to leave. It was assumed that any new husband worth his salt would support his spouse. The lady's new role as wife and (possibly) mother ruled out future employment. Such were the prevailing social attitudes of the era.

While their menfolk were away dealing with the Hun, this determined group of young ladies was drafted in to take charge of the upper and lower decks. In the event of an inebriated male passenger causing trouble for a conductress, the motorman, point iron in hand, would be called to issue summary justice to the offender. This was an effective way of maintaining law and order on the tramways!
LT Museum

As a result of the appalling casualties of the First World War, the Company did later revise its policy and war widows were employed as clerks in the Traffic Office and for general clerical tasks. The *TOT Staff Magazine* occasionally mentions Wedding Presentations in its columns. On 13th September 1929, Miss W. Dudley, a telephone operator at Manor House, was feted by her 'tramway friends and colleagues'. In his speech, one of the MET's electrical engineers, Mr P.M. Hunt, spoke of Miss Dudley's 'great tact and self control' before presenting her with a handsome canteen of cutlery.

On the engineering side of the MET organisation there were a number of skilled craftsmen and semi-skilled electrical staff to cope with the mechanical tasks of keeping the rolling stock maintained and the permanent way up to scratch. Jobs listed included fitters, turners, armature winders, carpenters, painters, body makers, washers, track cleaners, linesmen and clerks of work.

As described in Chapter 6, just before the First World War control of the MET passed from the British Electric Traction Company to the Combine. Tramway employees were set to benefit from this change of ownership, and in many respects the Combine became a model employer. Labour relations were generally good and rates of pay were above the national average for tramway workers. In contrast to the horsecar driver's sixty hour week, motormen were granted a six day, 48 hour week by the spring of 1922. Depot staff worked one hour less a week. The new contract stated that employees were entitled to eight days' annual paid leave. Overtime and Sunday rates were also adjusted. The agreement was sponsored by the National Joint Industrial Council for the Tramway Industry, and it came into effect from 17th April 1922. The hourly rate of remuneration was left for the employers to sort out.

By the time of the 1922 settlement most employees of the MET were members of the Transport and General Workers Union. Branch activity was handled by elected officials at each depot. In March 1924 a strike was called in response to the Combine's attempt to lower wages. In a letter dated 19th June 1923, C.J. Spencer had endeavoured to convince staff to take a pay cut. He justified his actions by writing: 'Owing to the large and rapidly increasing number of omnibuses which are working in the areas served by the tramways, the earnings of my company are being seriously affected and tend to become worse and worse'.

Unfortunately for Spencer the General Secretary of the Union was none other than the redoubtable Ernest Bevin, and he was having none of it. At a mass meeting of London tramwaymen in February 1924 the vote was taken to strike if no agreement was reached. A tense month of negotiations followed. At midnight on 20th March tram crews struck and the busmen came out in sympathy. The next day a Court of Inquiry was set up by the Minister of Transport. As the strike threatened to spread to Underground motormen, the Prime Minister, Ramsay MacDonald, got involved. Eight days into the industrial action a provisional settlement was reached and on the ninth day the tramwaymen voted to accept a weekly wage increase of six shillings (30p) for drivers and conductors, and four shillings (20p) for depot staff. The threatened pay cut had been quashed by ministerial decree.

To judge this award in context, it is interesting to learn that platform staff earned between sixty-five shillings (£3.25) and seventy-three shillings (£3.65) a week. These rates were below those paid to busmen. Their weekly wage averaged between four pounds six shillings (£4.30) and four pounds ten shillings (£4.50). By the time of the London Transport regime, when the last ex-MET line succumbed to trolleybuses, tramway staff had almost achieved pay parity with their central bus colleagues.

In his 1933 book *Socialisation and Transport*, Herbert Morrison gives an insider's view of events:

In 1924 the tramwaymen struck for better wages and the omnibus workers struck in sympathy. Whilst it is not officially admitted, part of the settlement conceding higher tramway wages which the then Labour Prime Minister, Mr Ramsay MacDonald, arranged with the London County Council and the Combine, was that legislation should be passed restricting omnibus operation in the London traffic area.

The trauma of 1924 was a jolt to the smooth running of the MET and the experience threatened to be repeated during the General Strike of May 1926. Most tram crews heeded their union's request to join the stoppage. Sporadic violence did break out in the metropolitan area, when volunteers were invited by hard pressed managements to have a go at running a service. Several of these attempts came to grief when confronted by a phalanx of angry strikers. Car 106 was caught in the firing line whilst stationed outside Hendon Depot. It was so severely damaged that it never returned to passenger service. Such were the feelings generated by the strike that it seems remarkable things settled down so well after the return to work. Victimisation was discouraged on both sides.

Industrial disputes can give a distorted picture; there was also a more positive side to the undertaking. In order to encourage an *esprit de corps* amongst the staff, a well run social organisation was established. News for employees was published in the *TOT Staff Magazine,* which first appeared in 1914 as a four page spread devoted to letters from soldiers at the Front. By 1915 four pages had expanded to twenty-six, and in 1922, at a price of one penny per monthly issue, it had achieved the status of a thirty-six page magazine covering current events, views and staff activities. In 1934 the LPTB took over the publication and renamed it *Pennyfare*. After the Second World War it became the *London Transport Magazine*; it lasted until March 1973.

Perhaps a true yardstick of any organisation is how it deals with its accidents and tragedies. Each issue of the *TOT Staff Magazine* carried staff obituaries that are poignant reminders of a time before antibiotics and modern surgical techniques. It makes grim reading when we are told that relatively young employees could succumb to pleurisy or influenza. In July 1930 an obituary notice was printed for Harry Creed, aged 19. He was a clerk in the Traffic Office at Manor House. He had joined the MET in 1925 at the age of 14 as an office messenger. At the other end of the age spectrum, the staff magazine of October 1930 regretted the demise of Driver H.L. Kenworthy of Edmonton Depot at the age of 73. He had spent 36 years in the service of the Company.

The matter of staff welfare also included the families of MET and other Combine workers. As reported in the *TOT Staff Magazine*, outings for mothers and children to benefit from the fresh air of the countryside were organised on a regular basis. One such took place on 12th August 1924, when a party of over 200 people was conveyed in three lavishly decorated tramcars from Hounslow LUT Depot to Folly Farm, Hadley Woods near Barnet. At the helm of the lead car was Motorman 'Uncle Ben' Davies. Much gratitude was expressed to MET staff and officials, who had contributed in no small measure to make the day a resounding success.

Every year the *TOT Staff Magazine* carried reports of trips organised for the families of the staff. Another such day out began early on the morning of 19th August 1931, when at 6.45am a party of just over 200 was conveyed by special trams from Finchley Depot to New Southgate Station. There they picked up an excursion train for Southend-on-Sea. Unfortunately, it was still raining at 9.45, when the party headed from Southend Station to the Kursaal. Around noon the rain abated. This break in the weather gave the children the opportunity to go on the boating lake. At 3.15pm Woolworths in the High Street laid on a special tea, following which the younger members of the party received their chocolates, a toy from the store and a stick of rock.

The highlight of the day was described as the sea trip on the new Princess of Wales pleasure boat. This carried the group across the mouth of the Thames to Sheerness Harbour, where the battleships HMS Repulse and HMS Valiant were at anchor. After being suitably impressed by the might of the Royal Navy, the pleasure boat returned everyone to Southend beach, where the kids had fun making sandcastles. It was noted that the party 'arrived back at Finchley at 10.30pm, tired but happy, after having spent a really good day in spite of the unkind weather'.

Christmas parties provided another high spot of the year. In complete contrast to the parsimony of the BET years, the Edmonton Depot staff laid on a sumptuous spread for 350 local children. According to the *TOT Staff Magazine* for February 1927, there were 'great piles of cakes and other good things for the little guests'. In addition to a packet of sweets and other 'novelties', each child was given a surprise gift of a souvenir mug, made for the occasion. On it was a picture of 'Daddy's tramcar with the words EDMONTON 1926 below'. After tea the children were kept amused by a ventriloquist and a conjurer. At half past seven the mums and dads arrived and the entertainment continued until 11pm.

In order to gauge the range of activities and benefits available to the average MET employee, one only has to choose a random copy of the *TOT Staff Magazine* to see what was on offer. In the March 1927 issue the Metropolitan Electric Tramways Athletic & Benevolent Club announced that the managing committee had awarded grants to two members so that they could recuperate at a convalescent home. In the days before the NHS and the Welfare State, time off for illness could have serious financial consequences for any family; hence this in-house insurance scheme was very welcome. The Combine opened Philbeach Convalescent Home in March 1925. It was situated at Hythe on the coast of Kent, and was used by women and children to give them a break from the daily grind of working class London life. Lady Ashfield, wife of the Chairman, took a particular interest in the welfare of those spending a week by the seaside. It was probably the only holiday some kids ever had.

Aside from the Benevolent Section of the March issue, there were reports from the Hendon Shops (Works) Branch on an interdepartmental billiards tournament. Results from a competition on the rifle range were also recorded. Manor House Branch noted the scores of several football matches involving MET employees. At Stonebridge Park they had just had a successful social evening, where their own band had been augmented by a string orchestra. Billiards, football and cricket also featured – in the case of the latter, potential recruits to the team were informed that practice matches would begin on 1st May.

In another article in the March magazine there was a report on a meeting of the TOT Radio Association. We are told that, with C.J. Spencer in the chair, 'there was a large and keenly interested audience, and the display by Messrs Peto-Scott, featuring the "All British Six" and the "Solodyne" one-dial receiver, was one of the finest yet seen at a T.O.T. radio meeting'.

One wonders what the members' reactions were, when at the end of the session, they were told that on 15th March 'Mr R.R. Peccorini has kindly consented to talk on Television'! This was an extremely advanced concept for 1927 and it is to the credit of General Manager Spencer and others in senior management that they fostered such an environment of scientific enquiry. The piece ends with a note that a number of LCC Tramways staff had applied to join the Radio Association.

Continuing the radio theme, the Company was not averse to gaining extra publicity by allowing employees to be interviewed by the new medium. In the April 1926 edition of the *TOT Staff Magazine* the following short piece appeared:

As our Wireless enthusiasts are doubtless aware, an interesting feature of the 2LO programme on 12th March was a talk on tramways by Inspector Curtis of the MET, who recounted the daily work of a driver and supplemented his talk by simple descriptions of many of the mechanical features of rolling stock and permanent way.

Combine employees, including several from the tramways section, were instrumental in persuading the BBC to broadcast a service from Central Hall, Westminster on Sunday, 15th January 1928. It was noted that a party of TOT men had previously visited the Savoy Hill studio of the BBC to make the necessary arrangements.

A more impromptu performance was reported in the staff magazine the previous month. In an age before ghetto blasters and intrusive muzak, it related how, to the delight of his fellow passengers, a young man on a MET tram had tuned his portable wireless receiver to the evening music programme of 2LO. The sound was 'of a cello in the hands of Casals' and could be heard distinctly above the noise of the car. It was claimed that this might be the first wireless concert on a moving public vehicle!

Representatives from the LCC Tramways were not only interested in the TOT Radio Association; they were also present at a gathering held in Acton Depot on 9th February. Again, General Manager Spencer presided over the proceedings. The topic this time was 'Tramways Improvements'. A full house came to hear Mr S.B. Hewitt, Mechanical Engineer, give a detailed account of the Combine's progress in updating its tramcars. Attention was firmly fixed on the relative merits of the two experimental cars – Bluebell, built at Hendon, and an, as yet unnamed vehicle, due to emerge from the Chiswick Works of the LGOC (this car later earned the nickname 'Poppy'). Mr Hewitt ended his talk by expressing pleasure at the attendance of the LCC visitors. He hoped 'the more they were together, the better they would be'. This sentiment sums up the desire for all London's tramway personnel to work towards a common goal of preserving their industry.

Trackwork is proceeding along Lordship Lane in March 1932. Much of the hard pick and shovel labouring of earlier days has now been replaced by pneumatic drills and other mechanical aids. These permanent way workers were just as vital to the MET's well being as the platform staff. They had to be on call in all weathers. Note that electric current to power the equipment is being taken directly from the tramway overhead wire.
LT Museum

An innovation which would have appealed to retired Inspector Davies, who was quoted earlier in this chapter, was the introduction in the autumn of 1928 of an all electric canteen at Edmonton Depot. It was always a management intention to provide refreshments 'at short notice and at reasonable prices' as well as general eating facilities for the staff. This overcame 'difficulties experienced by the staff at outside refreshment houses, owing to the variations of hours of relief'.

Members of the MET management seemed to have excelled themselves in this case. Seating was for 40 men in a hygienic environment. Meals that had been prepared and cooked were displayed in a 'new showcase with a sloping glazed top and glazed sliding doors, so that all food may be kept under cover and protected from dust and flies'. All this must have been the envy of less fortunate tram crews in other parts of the metropolis, who had no opportunity to take their meal breaks in such luxurious surroundings as were being provided at the Combine's tram depots.

We end this chapter with a couple of reminiscences as recorded by the London Transport staff magazine *Pennyfare*. Conductor E. Badcock of Hackney Depot recalled the fun and games that could happen when taking a tram over the boundary from MET rails to LCC conduit track:

It was funny! As my tram reached Stamford Hill, we proceeded to change from overhead to conduit. So I pulled the trolley pole round to the driver's end. It was so tense, that pole (and I so light), that as I hit the hook on the front of the tram, I went flying. I flew so high that I was unable to drop; and so I swayed, first to the near-side, then off-side. Before I descended I let a motor car pass under me. And there was the regulator (safe on the pavement, he!) shouting: "Look! The man on the flying trapeze!"

No Health & Safety inspectors or litigation lawyers for Conductor Badcock in those days – he just saw the funny side and then got on with the job!

Inspector Charles Mabbett of Finchley Depot gave an interview to *Pennyfare* in March 1945. His is one of the best summaries of the social benefits offered to MET staff:

. . . The Inspector enjoys the joke of saying that his first day on the trams was April Fool's Day 1905. Soon he saw the scope for promotion of good fellowship through the practice of recreation and philanthropy. As he says –

'I have taken an active part in the social side of the ex MET Athletic, Social and Benevolent Club: branch secretary at Finchley for a number of years and Benevolent Fund representative also.

'I've many happy memories of the early days: some of the happiest concern the Children's Summer Outings from Finchley Depot and the Christmas Parties held at Manor House Offices.

'I don't forget, either, the TOT Mutual Aid Fund of the first Great War and its service to the dependants of employees away in HM Forces. I don't forget those grand parties at the New Bohemia and Pound Lane Drill Hall, or the summer outings to Folly Farm, Barnet – to mention some of the treats for wives and children of those employees.

The opening of the tram route between Golders Green and North Finchley was a big event in Insp. Mabbett's career. He and Insp. Kirby assisted in the working of the new line, which, opened in December 1909, was started on the so called Fair Fare system – one farthing a section. From that date he worked nowhere but at Finchley Depot; he was there for 35 years, and his service totalled 40 years.

Cleaning staff employed in each tram depot were expected to do a thorough job. It was a matter of professional pride that no member of the fleet was sent out on the road in an unfit or dirty condition. The grime of London's streets is being washed off by a combination of a high pressure hose and an extendable window cleaning pole. *LT Museum*

Of course, there was much in each edition of the *TOT Magazine* to interest the other branches of the Combine – the Underground and the bus staff. Any objective observer would probably conclude that this was an organisation that cared about its workforce. Indeed, there seems to be so many activities on offer that the MET social events programme of the 1920s and early 1930s would put to shame many employers in the twenty-first century – especially those in the public transport business with a predilection for unwashed vehicles, whose staff live in daily fear of abusive passengers!

On 1st July 1933 the MET ceased to exist, but in many ways the ethos of the Combine survived. The MET system was incorporated into the London Passenger Transport Board. Rates of pay for tram drivers and conductors were standardised at seventy-three shillings (£3.65) per week, as opposed to eighty-six shillings and six-pence (£4.32) for a driver working in the Central Bus division. By January 1935, former MET motormen and conductors could expect to earn around seventy-five shillings (£3.75) per week. At the end of 1938, after the last ex-MET line had been converted to trolleybuses, the rate of pay had risen to eighty-two shillings (£4.10). The difference in wages between tramwaymen and their Central Bus colleagues was always a bone of contention. It was certainly true that bus crews in the central area were the favoured majority. Tram personnel had more flexible working arrange-ments than the men on the bus side of London Transport. In the circumstances, tramwaymen had every right to feel even more aggrieved about the disparity in pay. There was a feeling that the bus people were being pampered. It speaks volumes for the *esprit de corps* amongst the members of the tramway fraternity that they weath-ered the upheaval caused by the trolleybus conversion programme and did not join in the Central Bus strike of May 1937.

10. Fighting the Competition

As it faced the New Year of 1924 the MET, together with the rest of the London tramway industry, was in a precarious state. Postwar inflation had added to wage costs. Prices of raw materials urgently needed for track repair and highway upgrading had shot up alarmingly. The final nail in the coffin was the presence of pirate buses, whose effect on fare receipts was considerable. Clearly, something had to be done about unrestricted bus competition. As related in the previous chapter, a proposed wage cut triggered an all out strike. The Labour government then took notice, and as a result of pressure by both the Combine and the municipally run tramways, the London Traffic Act 1924 was duly passed into law on 7th August.

One of the Act's main provisions concerned the setting up of a Licensing Authority directly responsible to the Minister of Transport. Its main function was to sort out the public transport chaos on the roads of the capital. To this end it was empowered to enforce Restricted Streets Orders. In future all buses had to stick to Approved Routes. An operating licence could be refused if, in the opinion of the Minister and his advisers, 'that having regard to the service on any such route the maximum number of omnibuses to be used in maintaining the service is excessive'. This clause in the Act effectively stopped the pirates in their tracks.

The London Traffic Act breathed new life into the tramways, or, as one commentator gloomily put it, the Act granted them a stay of execution. As was widely expected, all tram routes in the capital were designated as restricted streets. The 1924 Act also led to the establishment of the London and Home Counties Traffic Advisory Committee, whose main task was to monitor congestion on the highways and byways of Greater London. It also had powers to enforce parking restrictions and to designate alternative routes for through traffic. Unfortunately, restrictions placed by local authorities and general lack of vision resulted in antiquated tramway track layouts being perpetuated. In spite of official parties being sent out and about in the world, many opportunities were missed. In North America and on the continent of Europe highway planners were active in the provision of passenger loading islands and traffic lanes, some of which were controlled by signalling systems – precursors of today's tram priority traffic lights.

As regards the MET, the Advisory Committee was particularly concerned to sort out the mess outside Finsbury Park Station. In its first annual report it suggested that local bus routes could be rearranged and that tram and bus stops could be repositioned so as to alleviate congestion at peak times. The 1925 Report confirmed that a revised list had been submitted to the Minister in April detailing some 600 streets along most of which tramway services were being operated.

In Woodhouse Road, North Finchley, the rivals are lined up for inspection. The General B Type bus was a great success and could transport passengers through areas of suburban and central London not served by tramways. The motorised taxicab is symbolic of future trends in private motoring. At this location today you would be hard put to find any trace of the MET tramways or their trolleybus successors, although the route 21 legacy lives on in the current 221 bus service. *LT Museum*

Although the MET and the London General Omnibus Company belonged to the same organisation, that did not stop the latter running competing services. Bus route 69 ran from Waltham Cross to Camberwell Green. Here in Fore Street, Edmonton, buses outnumber car 192.
D. Jones Collection

Seating capacities and loadings for trams and buses were studied on four different routes. One of these was the MET line between the tram terminus, Horn Lane, Acton and Tally Ho Corner, North Finchley. The figures were recorded on 11th and 12th August 1925; they reveal that the highest seat occupancy was 45% on north-bound cars between seven and eight in the morning. This was disappointing, bearing in mind that LCC, West Ham and East Ham cars on the trunk service from Aldgate to Barking managed a figure of almost 80% capacity. In fact, out of all seven routes surveyed, the two Combine tram services had the poorest results.

The findings of the 1925 Report cannot have gone unnoticed by Lord Ashfield and his fellow directors. However, although the state of the MET was of concern, it was not yet a top priority. As we shall see, the bigwigs of the Combine were astute political operators and they correctly decided that, whatever fate befell the MET, the Middlesex County Council would continue to support an asset in which so much ratepayers' money was invested.

One can only speculate that, at this time in the mid 1920s, the attention of the Combine was drawn to improving bus services, now that the big boys had effectively seen off the competition from the pirates. Another enormous headache was the disastrous financial performance of the London United lines. Clearly, the prospect of trying to maintain antiquated rolling stock operating over disintegrating tracks was not an enticing one. Several solutions to the problem were put forward. The idea of a common fund for passenger transport in the Greater London area was floated amongst politicians, but any agreement to pool resources would take some years to become a reality. In the meantime, the tramways operated by the Combine had to continue to function after a fashion. Replacement by LGOC buses was not considered feasible at this time. Modernising the best bits of the three tram systems was an option, as was a policy of make do and mend, until a new London wide transport operator could be found. The fact that the MET survived and confounded its critics is due in no small measure to the courage and vision of General Manager C.J. Spencer.

Christopher John Spencer was born in 1876 and received an early initiation into the world of electric tramways as an apprentice of the Blackpool Electric Tramway Company, whose first line had opened on 29th September 1885. From Blackpool he moved on to the South Staffordshire system. In 1898 he was appointed General Manager at Bradford. After a successful career in West Yorkshire he joined the war effort as an assistant to the Admiralty and it was here that he was headhunted for the post of General Manager of the Combine's tramway operations. He can be characterised as a tram man through and through; he played a very active role in metropolitan and national discussions on the future of tramways. His views on tramcar modernisation sparked debate among his fellow managers and rolling stock engineers. Much was recorded in contemporary trade journals, such as the *Tramway & Railway World*.

After a visit to North America in 1920, C.J. Spencer outlined his views to the Congress of the Tramways and Light Railways Association. In his lecture he pointed out that the arrested development of British tramcar design had indeed led managers to think in narrow tramlines. This type of parochialism, he opined, would be fatal for tramway operators if it went unchecked. He was certain that advances in motor bus design, coupled with the evolving technology of the heavy oil (diesel) engine, could be matched by similar improvements in the tramway world. He suggested the development of lightweight vehicles might go hand in hand with the introduction of one man operated trams.

One of the MET Type E cars had already been converted to one man operation and was working on the Tolworth to Richmond Park Gates route of the London United. It had been rebuilt with a front entrance/exit; an automatic ticket machine assisted the driver in cutting waiting time at stops. Results from this experiment had convinced Spencer that any improvement in tram design, especially with regards to the position of staircases and entrances, would depend on what method of fare collection was employed. Furthermore, passenger comfort could be guaranteed by installing upholstered seats; improved service to the public would ultimately demand faster trams. On the latter point it is worth quoting from the transcript of his lecture notes to the Congress:

An average speed of 7 to 7½mph is quite common, but it is in reality a poor performance for a vehicle with an almost unlimited amount of power at its disposal. This is a matter that has had some attention at the undertakings in London, and it might interest the members to know that the MET Tramways, for example, has an average speed, including all lay-over time, of 9.19mph, with consequent beneficial effects on costs and usefulness of service, but I think even that figure could be improved with newer equipments.

From a modern day standpoint an average speed approaching 10 mph (16 km/h) for a public transport vehicle crossing London seems impressive, and by the standards of 21st century traffic congestion, almost unobtainable! However, Spencer wasn't finished in his campaign. He envisaged new tracks on which even higher speeds would be possible. Segregated rights of way adjacent to existing highways would ensure reliability of operation and would go some way to counteract anti-tram propaganda put out by motoring organisations. Also on the agenda was the provision of interchange stations where passengers from the Combine's tube lines and bus routes could transfer easily to the trams. The MET General Manager even persuaded

Illegal races and incidents with competing independent buses could sometimes end in disaster. In November 1929 this car came to grief on Edgware Road. Note the wonderful array of 'spare parts' shed by the stricken tramcar. For some reason a member of the maintenance crew has replaced the trolley pole on the overhead wire. *D. Jones Collection*

Middlesex County Council to include extra tramway powers in a Parliamentary Bill they were promoting in 1925. This would give the MCC the right to 'alter the position of any light railway or tramway so that the track shall be separate from the carriageway'. Unfortunately for Londoners, none of these express transit schemes came to fruition.

In the same year that the MCC Bill appeared, Spencer again went on the offensive, and such was his drawing power, that at a meeting in Acton held on 4th November, late arrivals had to stand at the back of the hall. His topic was 'The Tramway position in London: What the Management is doing and what the Staff can do' – and he began by stating the current position of 331 route miles (532 km) over which 2,800 cars operated. The Combine lines carried 18.5% of the tramway traffic. Middlesex County Council had invested some two million pounds into the MET undertaking and 'it was out of the question' that the tramways would be abandoned. All that was wanted was fair play in respect of unnecessary and unwarranted bus competition. Spencer was of the opinion that extravagant services provided by bus companies would eventually have to be paid for by the passenger. On the tram side he foresaw little profit or no profit at all until the provisions of the 1924 Act were fully implemented. Eighteen percent of the MET's passenger traffic was carried at workmen's fares. The company had never yet had an adequate return on its capital. The balance of profit had fallen each year since 1922 and there would be a deficit again this year (1925).

One central tenet of the General Manager's philosophy was that no other vehicle could shift crowds like the tram. At peak times large numbers of passengers could be transported quickly with the minimum of fuss. He repeated his belief that segregated tracks and loading islands would add to the efficiency of the operation. At the end of the lecture 'a very interesting discussion took place, a number of Inspectors, Motormen and Conductors expressing their views'.

There is no doubt that C.J. Spencer was looked on as an inspirational leader by his own workforce, but his high profile in tramway circles did have its negative side. Although a consummate diplomat, he sometimes let the mask slip. The dead hand of the LCC and its effect on joint services irritated him. What can only be termed professional jealousy manifested itself among certain of his contemporaries. When the LCC later brought out their new E/3 and HR/2 classes, Spencer quite rightly referred to them as 'one step forward, two steps backward' in tramcar design. To him they represented the triumph of conservatism over progressive thinking. By the time of the appearance of LCC car 1, Bluebird, in 1932, relations between the MET General Manager and the LCC's Chief Rolling Stock Engineer had improved somewhat. But that is to get ahead of our story.

Outright opponents of Spencer's tram modernising philosophy had in their ranks Lord Montagu of Beaulieu, a vocal member of the House of Lords motoring lobby. A clutch of transport managers, including such notables as R. Stuart Pilcher, Manchester transport boss and sometime President of the Municipal Tramways and Transport Association, were convinced that their only salvation lay with the bus or the trolleybus. To these people the quick and easy solution lay in scrapping the trams, not building new ones.

Through the columns of the *TOT Staff Magazine* Combine employees were kept informed of the progress of Mr Spencer's modernisation plans. An inkling of what was to come appeared in the September 1925 issue, when an article headed *Tramcar Comfort* heralded the start of a major renovation programme. The gist of the account was that the Tramways Sections of the TOT had entered into friendly rivalry with their confrères in the Underground and the London General Omnibus Company in devising new standards of comfort in urban locomotion. Although only a handful of LUT vehicles had been upgraded, the tone of the article leaves readers in no doubt what to expect in the future – the tramways would be fighting back to regain lost ground.

Further evidence of the tramway revival is contained in a report on a lecture given by the Tramways Technical Assistant, L.B. Hewitt, at Fulham Town Hall, on 19th October 1925. Frank Pick, one of the leading lights of the Combine, chaired the meeting, which was intended to give a boost to staff morale. An unnamed reporter gives us a snapshot of the pep talk:

. . . L.B. Hewitt's paper dealt with recent improvements on the lines of the London and Suburban Traction Company. In street traction speed was a valuable asset, and the equipment of part of the L & ST fleet with new high power motors and improved brakes had given excellent results . . . The latest type of magnetic brake in use was probably the most powerful that had been fitted to any road vehicle. It had the drawback, however, of causing rather severe wear to the rails. On tramways speed was regulated by law in accordance with the peculiarities of the various sections of line, and recently the Ministry of Transport had authorised certain increases of speed on the MET system, the maximum having been raised from 16mph to 20mph.

. . . The new types of double deck cars, with upholstered seats on top, described in a recent issue of TOT Magazine, and improvements in overhead construction and permanent way repair plant, were treated by Mr Hewitt. The addition of a small percentage of cadmium to the copper from which the trolley wire is drawn had the effect of lengthening the life of this important item in tramway operation by about 200 per cent.

Mention of overhead wiring confirms the attention to detail of Spencer and his team. It was typical that even the chemical composition of trolley wire should come under scrutiny, so that costs could be brought under control. To the management and engineering team all elements had to come together to produce a successful whole – it was obvious that faster trams required better maintained tracks and overhead equipment. In the latter field experiments had been going on since 1921 on the relative merits of trolley skids (as later used on trolleybuses) versus conventional trolley wheels. In 1927 further research to minimise the risk of dewirements resulted in car 3 being equipped with a Fischer bow collector, of a type which subsequently found favour with Glasgow and several other British cities. For the sake of comparison, car 34 received a Siemens designed bow collector. Tests using both vehicles were inconclusive. Because of through running agreements, any mass conversion of the fleet depended on the attitude of the LCC. Although they, too, carried out experiments with bows and pantographs on the Downham to Grove Park section, trolley poles were destined to remain as standard on all vehicles.

Bow collectors were popular on the Continent of Europe and they found some favour with British operators from the late 1920s onwards. This is a close up of the MET experimental rig.

The leading article in the *Tramway & Railway World* for 18th February 1926 described the improved cars on the MET that had been introduced to service 29. Passengers travelling on the Enfield to Euston route had the opportunity to sample well sprung seats, upholstered in fawn and blue moquette. Interior lighting in each of the six upgraded vehicles was some fifty per cent brighter than in the rest of the fleet. Experimental use by conductors of the Aspinall Ticket Machine was expected to speed up the process of fare collection. We are told that the machine held 250 tickets in a continuous strip and that replacement of the ticket pack was straightforward.

Although the advent of the May General Strike had hampered progress, passenger figures for August Bank Holiday credited the Combine's tramways with shifting a total of 1,608,626 people over the extended weekend. Slowly but surely, things seemed to be getting back on track.

The next big event in the MET calendar was the unveiling in 1927 of two experimental tramcars. Cars 318 and 319 have already been described in the rolling stock chapter. C.J. Spencer was lauded by the public relations people as one tramway chief who wanted to buck the trend against tramways. Here was someone who believed in a revolution in tramcars and, moreover, he seemed to have the genius to motivate the works staff.

Progress on the rolling stock front rather masked what was going on in behind the scenes in the troubled relationship between the MET and the County Council. It may have come as a shock to many, when they read in the September 1926 Editorial of the *Tramway & Railway World*:

For six years negotiations have been going on between the Council and the company concerning the granting of a new lease for the tramways. In the meantime the Council has refused to put the roads into a state of proper repair unless the tramway track be repaired at the same time. Another interesting development of the situation is the decision of the County Council to force a settlement of the debt owing by the tramways company under a threat of legal proceedings. The tramways were constructed by the Middlesex County Council, who leased them to the Metropolitan Electric Tramways Company at an annual charge of five per cent on the Council's outlay on construction plus 45 per cent of the gross revenue as rent. The seriousness of the position may be judged by the fact that for fifteen years no rent has been paid, while the tramway undertaking, by reason of its financial position, has not been able to keep the track in repair as stipulated in the lease. At a recent meeting of the County Council it was stated that the Tramway Company are willing to enter into negotiations for the surrender of their lease.

Hints of bankruptcy and repossession by the MCC must have made unpleasant reading for some in Combine HQ. No mention was made in the text of support from other members of the group; the reader of the Editorial is left with the impression that the MET would be left to sort out its own mess. Furthermore, the atmosphere generated by this uncertainty was calculated to curtail investment plans in rolling stock and new infrastructure.

Needless to say, there was another agenda to all this backstairs activity; there were any number of political games going on. After all, what would the County Council do, if Lord Ashfield and his fellow directors just handed back the lease? The prospect of paddling their own canoe alarmed many at the MCC. Discreet enquiries conducted by some Middlesex county councillors with their opposite numbers on the LCC produced a negative response – one county council did not want to take over another's lame duck. The LCC had rescued the Leyton system from near collapse on 1st July 1921, and, having learnt from experience, it was unwilling to strike further deals with its neighbours.

Over a period of six years, the problem of the renewal of the tramways lease was batted back and forth like a shuttlecock. At one point the MCC gave the Combine an ultimatum that a new financial agreement between the parties had to be concluded by 31st December 1927 or the County Council would run the system itself. This deadline came and went. Eventually a deal was struck. An important factor in the negotiations with the County Council was the Company's acknowledged commitment to improving rolling stock and services. An annual fixed rent of £62,221 was agreed together with a new 42 year lease. However, nothing was written on tablets of stone. It was an open question how long the arrangement would last, before all public transport in London was amalgamated into one organisation.

11. Mr Spencer's Pride and Joy

Christopher John Spencer's ideas on tramcar design were based on first hand experience of tramway operation in the UK. The appearance of the Feltham type tram, regarded by many transport historians as one of the finest vehicles ever to grace the streets of London, was a direct result of this research. The Feltham can lay claim to being an icon of British tramway technology. However, in spite of this iconic status, it can be argued that, although a great success on certain Metropolitan Electric and London United routes, the new design failed to halt the decline of London's tramways.

Spencer had had the chance to take part in study tours on the Continent of Europe and in North America. Time and again he hammered home his belief that a truly modern tramcar could outperform its rivals in the passenger transport world. In order to achieve this goal, higher service speeds were essential; vehicles of lightweight body construction should be equipped with comfortable transverse seats; separate entrances and exits would cut out time lost at stops; air brakes should be fitted together with conventional magnetic track brakes. As regards the issue of whether a single deck car was to be preferred, Spencer rather bowed to the tradition that the travelling public in Britain was accustomed to double deckers, and therefore, he declined to follow his American and European colleagues in promoting large fleets of high capacity single deck trams.

In a speech to the Tramways and Light Railways Association Conference at Torquay in July 1926, C.J. Spencer set out his stall:

I should like to see the day when we have a really modern tramcar – we have not seen it yet, but I think we shall soon – and so far as my own undertaking in London is concerned, it may be of interest to you to know that we have been experimenting with reconditioning our cars by putting in high speed motors, cross seats, and other things which we can possibly persuade our directors to allow us to do; and it was not always easy, because raising money for tramways is a difficult operation in these days . . .

The London County Council and the Metropolitan Tramways have a higher speed than any tramcars in the world, and in order to prevent any misunderstanding, I would like to point out that the speed of tramcars in London is higher than the average speed of the omnibuses . . .

Very great advantages arise by having tramcars which I will call of the circulating type, where passengers get on at one end and get off at the other, allowing a car to be loaded and unloaded simultaneously. It is very convenient in the first place, and the passengers like it. But what is of greatest importance is that it saves time, and every second saved on the schedule means money . . .

Car 320 is pictured at Golders Green when on proving runs in public service. The contrast between this vehicle and its predecessor, car 319 Poppy, is quite startling. Lack of conduit gear prevented its being shown off in joint services with the LCC. *LT Museum*

When I was in America recently, I was immensely impressed by these American cars on the pay-as-you-enter principle. But there is a great and essential difference between the American system and our system, because they have a flat basis of fare. There is no question of issuing a ticket. A passenger gets on to the car and drops his nickel into the box and passes to his seat. I should like to see something of that sort in this country, but I am afraid it would not be looked upon as practical here . . .

With regard to the air brake, that is a very fine brake, and I have instinctive leanings towards it. Although we are using the magnetic brake in London, frankly I do not like it. It is a rough brake. But at the same time I cannot overlook the fact that the higher average speeds which we are able to run in London as contrasted with many other places are due to the magnetic brake.

Even a cursory reading of his speech emphasises the point that C.J. Spencer's ideas were decades in advance of contemporary thinking – trams with multiple doors, good average speeds and efficient braking systems operating in an environment with flat fares and even ticketless, pre-paid travel – all concepts with which we are familiar in the 21st century, but they must have seemed quite alien to most of the delegates at the Torquay conference.

Spencer's revolutionary new trams were destined to be built by the Union Construction Company of Feltham, Middlesex. The UCC was founded on 16th October 1901, under the direction of Charles Tyson Yerkes, an American transit tycoon. The original objectives of the enterprise encompassed a wide range from the promotion and construction of electric railways to the building and equipping of rolling stock. It was with this latter sphere of manufacture in mind that the semi-dormant operation of the company was revived in 1926, when modernisation of tube railway carriages was begun at the UCC. The works were situated off Victoria Road in Feltham, and in the period 1928–1930, they gained a full order book to construct 95 underground railway motor units, 86 control trailer carriages and 54 unpowered trailer units.

To all intents and purposes the UCC was an integral part of the Combine, and therefore, it was not surprising that its expertise was also exploited in the tramway field. Leaving aside the Southmet, which was not a serious contender for fleet modernisation, the two major candidates for UCC attention were the MET and the LUT. Costs were kept down by keeping the research and development of new tramcars in house. Economies could also be made by using jigs, fittings and lightweight construction materials that were already on site in connection with new tube rolling stock.

After close supervision by C.J. Spencer of the initial stages of the project, three models of a brand new class of tramcar were set to emerge from the works. First up on the list was car 320, christened "Blossom" by the staff; the vehicle was an instant front page success with the technical press. With the headline 'Notable Achievement by the Tramways Management of the London Underground Group', the *Tramway & Railway World* April 1929 devoted a number of pages to the Super Pullman Car:

The new car thus evolved may be said to constitute a model for the world in four directions, viz., maximum comfort, speedy and silent running, suitability for dealing with mass traffic by means of a rear entrance, front exit, and capacious enclosed platforms, and an especially pleasing exterior. All this has been achieved at a total weight of 16.75 tons with four motor propulsion, an increase in weight of only 4 cwt. over the old type of car with its two motors . . .

Its popularity should be very great, for it gives luxurious riding, while its appearance is graceful on account of streamline effects. The passenger's comfort is enhanced both sitting and standing. The slightly larger dimensions of the new car enable the occupants of seats to sit without knees coming into contact with the backs of seats, and in both saloons there are double seats on each side of the gangway. The commodious enclosed platforms have doorways sufficiently wide to permit of more than one person entering or leaving at the same time. The extra area of the platforms is in accordance with worldwide practice for dealing with rush traffic and at other times permitting short distance riders to stand if they so desire . . .

On boarding the car, the impression is at once obtained of comfort, light and general airiness in the lower saloon. The wider car allows two transverse seats of ample comfort, giving adequate elbow room . . . The top saloon is a triumph that reflects especial credit on the designers. It is entirely unobstructed along its whole length of something like 39 feet, giving free movement for passengers around the staircases, and providing seats equally luxurious to those of the lower saloon . . .

Chromium plating is used for all other visible fittings. The interiors of the saloons have been designed as free as possible from all moulding or corners which would be liable to collect dirt, and the colouring has been selected to give a bright and harmonious appearance, due regard being paid to serviceability. All interior panels are of silver grey wood, and the ceilings are of stippled Sundeala. All floors are covered with cork carpet . . .

The introduction of the Super Pullman car does not exhaust the story of enterprise shown by the Companies. For two years the management has been pursuing a policy of reconditioning and remodelling the rolling stock . . . That the public appreciate this forward move was shown by the fact that in 1928 the number of passengers carried totalled 192,867,000 as compared with 180,800,000 in 1927, an increase of seven per cent.

In this line up of the two prototypes only minor differences in bodywork are apparent. In theory, car 330 could traverse the whole London system because it was equipped with plough gear. In practice, the length and width of all three Feltham prototypes (and the succeeding production batch) would rule out their use on many sections of the future London Transport tramway network, where tight curves and restricted clearances abounded. *LT Museum*

The modernity of Spencer's car 320 was very apparent when compared with the latest offering from the LCC. Their new HR prototype, which occupied the next couple of pages in the April issue, looked distinctly old fashioned and out of touch with the new trends in tramway technology.

Employees of the MET/LUT and the UCC were sworn to secrecy until the official unveiling of the next prototype, car 330. The Press Bureau, Underground Railway, 55 Broadway, SW1 issued a comprehensive handbook entitled *Specimen Cars for the Metropolitan Electric Tramways*. In content and layout the handbook was obviously aimed at professionals in the public transport industry. As such, an objective observer might have thought that the UCC was anxious to obtain further orders from outside the Combine. However, as we shall see, it was never really intended that the UCC should set up in competition with Brush at Loughborough or English Electric at Preston as a major tramcar manufacturer. Certain design features of centre entrance car 331 were later patented and licensed to English Electric.

The background to the construction of both prototypes was set out in the text. Most of the handbook was devoted to technical details, and one of the main drawings is illustrated below. A major part of the text attempted to explain how weight savings on experimental cars 320 and 330 had been obtained through the extensive use of aluminium alloys. The handbook claimed that further benefits accruing from this choice of construction material included reduced power consumption, less wear and tear due to lighter car parts and lower lubrication costs. This in turn meant that higher schedule speeds could be obtained, with the added bonus of lower expenditure on track maintenance.

Obvious differences between cars 320 and 330 included truck design and position of the two staircases. Car 320 was lettered with the full company name just above the lower deck windows, whilst car 330 received the newest METROPOLITAN transfer in a style that would later become familiar with London Transport after 1934.

Drawing of 330. This and 320 were very similar in terms of bodywork. No. 330 was equipped with maximum traction bogies.

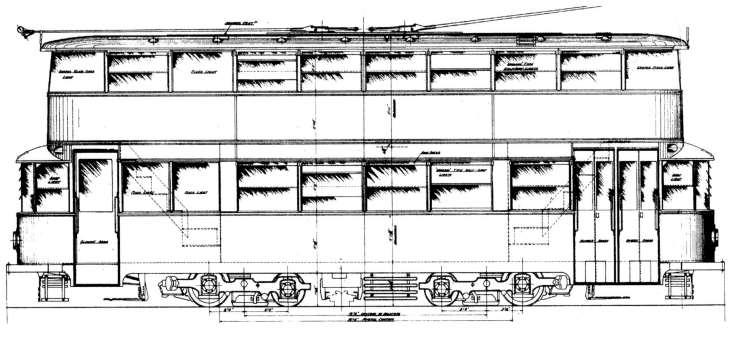

Rather annoyingly, as far as the UCC was concerned, the specifications for car 330's trucks were changed at a late stage – obviously there had been 'words' between Spencer and the design team at Feltham. This resulted in important alterations to the underframe of the car. It was noted that if further vehicles of the same design were required, the whole underframe and load carrying points above the bogies would have to be redesigned.

The *Tramway & Railway World* for 21st November 1929 gave a glowing report of yet another MET debutante. Headed – 'Pay-As-You-Pass System on the Metropolitan Electric Tramways. An Experimental Car Designed to Increase Speed and Comfort' – the article suggested that the tramways management of the Combine had taken another step towards the eventual adoption, as standard, of the passenger flow method of tramcar construction.

Whether there is to be a machine issue of tickets or a continuance of the bell-punch system is a question which will be decided by experience with the new car, but it should be noted that the ticket machine has to be operated by the conductor, who is seated in a recess by the side of the saloon. Both methods were adopted on a trial run made by the car on 6th November between Golders Green and the North Finchley depot . . .

In view of the adverse reports that have followed attempts at introducing electric heating on an extensive southern tramway undertaking, it is of interest to note that the new car has an electric radiator on each platform. It is installed in the louvred door of a cabinet which occupies the space under the staircase. In the cabinet are the motor resistances, sand hoppers and air engines operating the exit doors . . . The lighting at night is brilliant. Each saloon has sixteen frosted bulbs with vitreous enamel reflectors, giving a soft light with high visibility and an elimination of shadow. A special dipping headlight is fitted on the front of each dash . . .

The controllers are the British Thomson Houston Company's type B527B, and the two 60 hp 509 motors are by the same makers . . . The motorman is allowed discretion as to which brake he uses . . . in practice the air brake, which does not cause rail wear, is used for the ordinary service stops and the magnetic for emergency. The magnetic brake has several attractive features. One is that it is less likely to cause skidding . . .

With the exception of interior finish, the body is a metal structure throughout. The car is designed with a low centre of gravity, and the platform and lower saloon are on the same level . . . In order to deaden noise and drumming induced in the car due to traffic conditions, the aluminium waist panels, quarter panels and roof panels have been lined on the inside with a loosely woven open mesh canvas.

Both cars experienced teething problems. Lord Ashfield, accompanied by members of the Combine board, made an official journey on 4th October 1929 to Finchley Depot in order to inspect his latest assets. Car 320 was working on the Whetstone to Cricklewood service 40 from May 1929. Sister car 330 had a couple of false starts necessitating at least one return trip to the LUT depot at Fulwell, so that the engineers there could fix several technical glitches. The car was fitted with a standard LCC plough carrier attached to the underframe of the lower saloon.

Car 330 was also allocated to service 40. It ran initially on the PAYP principle of fare collection, with a seated conductor, who issued tickets from a machine. However, tests proved that a conventional roving conductor was more efficient at coping with the complexities of the traditional British stage fare system. The Pay-As-You-Pass experiment was deemed a failure.

An interesting experiment was later tried on car 320 when a 'Radiovisor Step Indicator' was fitted to warn the motorman of the presence of a passenger on the rear step. The *TOT Staff Magazine* for November 1930 gave the following account:

A focused beam of light is projected across the front of the step of the tramcar and reflected back across the rear of the step on to a light sensitive selenium bridge. Interruption of the light beam due to a passenger boarding or alighting from the car increases the resistance of the selenium bridge, is amplified, and finally operates an electromagnetic relay, which in turn, short circuits the green ALL CLEAR light in the driver's cabin and displays a red warning light.

This somewhat rudimentary equipment failed to live up to expectations and it was removed. However, it is probably fanciful to speculate what might have happened, had Spencer and his team persevered with their experiments in amplified light beams – the boffins at the MET might have invented the first laser!

The final vehicle of the trio of experimentals is the well known car 331 "Cissie" – happily still with us and an active performer at the National Tramway Museum in Crich, Derbyshire. The car was always considered a pet project with C.J. Spencer to try out his theories regarding centre entrance trams. Interlock safety mechanisms prevented the doors opening whilst the car was in motion and the interior furnishings of the tram reflected experience gained with the previous two prototype vehicles. Car 331 ran on equal wheel trucks equipped with four 35 hp lightweight motors. Due to the position of the centre entrance steps it was impossible to fit a plough carrier.

Car 331 started work on the Whetstone to Cricklewood service in December 1930. It soon showed its efficiency in moving large numbers of rush hour passengers from Golders Green Station to North Finchley. Often the car was so crowded that a separate conductor was employed by the MET to collect fares on the top deck. Large numbers of standing passengers could also be transported.

A production order for one hundred trams of Type UCC was divided between the MET and the LUT. The Middlesex County Council was informed that 54 such vehicles would be acquired for the Metropolitan Electric fleet. The MET Felthams were fitted with plough carriers, so that they could work over LCC conduit tracks. Experience gained from the three prototypes helped settle the final design of the production batch. Although the passenger flow idea of using separate entrance and exit doors was retained, car 331's centre entrance/exit found no further favour.

The body shell of each Feltham was finished at the works and then towed on a trailer over to Fulwell Depot. Here it was fitted out mechanically and electrically. Each vehicle was equipped with two 70 hp traction motors, and ran on maximum traction trucks. In order to ensure safety of operation, rheostatic, magnetic track and air brakes were supplied as standard.

As part of the testing of the new car, trials were conducted along the Southbury Road tramway on Christmas Day 1930. One must assume that this was the only day in the year that the police could shut off the road in order to allow a 'race' between an LUT Feltham and an MET Feltham. The LUT cars had different motors and controllers from their MET sisters. Sandbags took the place of human beings in both saloons of the competing trams. It is not recorded what the local residents really thought as they sat down to their Christmas dinners. No doubt, some youngsters managed to tear themselves away from their presents to cheer on the contestants – anecdotal evidence indicates that the MET car won!

This view of MET car 331 at the National Tramway Museum, Crich, Derbyshire serves to emphasise the modernity of the design of this centre entrance tramcar. The museum staff and the many fundraisers are to be congratulated on a splendid restoration job. One minor quibble – in reality this car could not have worked over LCC conduit track to Holborn.

On 1st February 1931 Finchley Depot provided Felthams for service 40 between Whetstone and Cricklewood. They operated a mixed service with older, re-motored cars. Subsequently Wood Green Depot was favoured with an allocation of the new vehicles. Type UCC cars also operated on services 21 and 29. One obvious drawback was that the Felthams, with their greater width and length, could not operate over the whole system. Restrictive clearances on curves and at certain depots prevented their use on some potentially lucrative joint services.

W.H. Shaw, General Traffic Superintendent of the Combine tramways, gave an honest assessment of the Felthams in a paper read to the Congress of the Tramways, Light Railways and Transport Association in 1932. What is interesting about the following lecture is the implication that, although the Type UCC cars represented one exciting stage in tramcar development, there were still further new ideas in the pipeline. Mr Shaw admitted that the Felthams were not the last word – the engineers were thinking of 'something different for tomorrow' – but the UCC Type cars had had remarkably few problems in day-to-day operation:

The UCC car designers and their advisers started out to design a car which, being of quite reasonable dimensions for a road vehicle, ignored the regulations. A bold policy, and it succeeded in giving us a tramcar very much nearer the ideal and traffic requirements – a high degree of comfort for the slack hours with capacity in the rush. The principle must be the right one. So long, as in London, the omnibuses in their wisdom leave the workmen's traffic untouched so long must there be a large capacity vehicle to carry those crowds. But we must attract the slack hour traffic to enable us to live to do it.

The lower deck of car 355 provides some indication of the comfortable passenger accommodation. Smoking was not permitted in the lower saloon. The seats were covered in stylish moquette and were well upholstered. When the Felthams were first introduced, it was not unknown for homebound commuters from central London to nod off in the warmth of the lower deck. The purring of the motors, the gentle sway on the rails, plus the complete lack of petrol/diesel fumes, all contributed to their feeling of well being. Conductors usually used their discretion in alerting them, when their stop came in sight.
LT Museum

The balcony seat of car 330 offers a fine view of the road ahead, and, as such, it was a favourite for children as they explored their surroundings.
LT Museum

Normally our cars carry a maximum load on two, perhaps three half journeys a day. The seating capacity in the lower saloon of the UCC Type cars is 22, and in the upper saloon 42, a total of 64, which is ample for the non-rush periods. Capacity is obtained by the big platforms licensed to carry ten people standing at each end, giving a total capacity of 84. This number allows plenty of room for the conductor to pass between. On occasions of big football or other large crowds they carry more, and the capacity of the car is increased to about 100 (unofficially)!

For this and other reasons, I would like to have had bow collectors which turn automatically, though the two trolleys which are fitted are an advantage; they keep the car lighted when turning, and save time – except when the leading one jumps off its hook and hits a railway bridge. I know it is probably due to the conductor not getting the boom under the hook properly, but how, in the dark, is he to know? It would be interesting to know if other undertakings who operate with two trolleys have experienced this trouble occasionally and what steps have been taken to eliminate it.

I have no complaint against the air operated front exit door which works well and quickly, although the steel flap which drops to cover the space between the platform and the step is noisy, which is a pity because in all other respects the cars are very quiet. This front exit brings in its train the Ministry of Transport and their wants – a rear caution sign and a front door sign. Why a rear caution sign on these particular cars I do not know and it does not seem to have been definitely decided if it is a warning that the car is stopping, or a warning that passengers are alighting.

The front exit door has been fitted with a red flap made of stiff rubber about 12 ins. long and 4 ins. wide, which sticks out automatically as the door is opened and has STOP on it. It is a considerable safeguard, but the Ministry say we are too peremptory – it is not our job to say STOP to anyone. Life is full of little troubles when a Ministry is interested.

The air brake makes a delightfully smooth stop and if all cars were fitted it would, I am sure, save considerable expense and the irritation caused by renewal of rails at "all car" stops. It was anticipated that the motormen, after many years of use of the magnetic brake for service stops, would continue to use it on these cars to which it is fitted for emergency use only, but that did not happen. Owing to the efficiency and ease of application of the air brake only very few men did not 'cotton on' to it straightaway.

On the two routes which were completely equipped with the new cars the first showed an increase of 2 per cent on the same mileage and the second an increase of 6 per cent, and in spite of the general slump these receipts were maintained and are amongst the few routes showing increases. These routes ran 20 and 30 cars per hour in the peak and 15 and 18 in the slack hours, and the cars they replaced were not doddering old things with wooden seats, but fast and cross seated. The new cars with their quick acceleration and high speeds and smooth quick stopping air brakes enabled the company to cut running times by 8 to 10 per cent over the areas where they operated alone.

The last paragraph explains better than any words of the present author why the Felthams were such a success. C.J. Spencer and his design team could be very proud of their achievements.

To sum up, these UCC cars from the point of view of the traffic department are a success. Even if they had no operating advantages at all I contend their publicity value is considerable and well worth while. They have shown the public that tramways are not hidebound by tradition. In my opinion it is useless to alter the interior of the car only. It is the man in the street who never rides on a tram one wants to get, and to do that you have got to hit him in the eye with something new. He rides on one out of curiosity, he finds it comfortable, fast, smooth running and very well lighted. He continues to ride on them – their object is achieved.

Although the early 1930s fashions look dated, the message conveyed by this MET Feltham is timeless. Passengers boarding at Holborn were offered cheap fares and frequent services in comfortable, pollution free vehicles, with a conductor on hand to keep an eye on things. The Felthams supplied a quality of travel unmatched by the replacing trolleybuses and diesel buses. *LT Museum*

It was business as usual at Finsbury Park right up to the takeover by London Transport. Note the white armbands worn by the conductor of car 302. When he stretched out his arm to warn of an impending stop, they served as a safety warning for following motorists. *LT Museum*

12. METROPOLITAN TWILIGHT

Over the decades of the twentieth century many working Londoners have used their free time to get out of the 'smoke' to explore the surrounding countryside. All public transport providers in the capital were well aware that at weekends and on Bank Holidays they would have to cater for extra numbers of passengers. The public relations people at the Combine were particularly keen to promote their network of underground railways and motor buses. To this end they produced some attractive publicity material to encourage members of the public to travel out into the Greater London area. Colourful posters and advertisements harped on the benefits of country walks through unspoilt countryside, where the jaded city dweller could revive his spirits by enjoying the charm of rustic villages, with the added incentive of a thirst quenching pint at an olde worlde inn. Of course, all the recommended hikes along lanes, by hedgerows and across woods and fields began and ended at a station or a bus terminus. The era of mass private motoring had yet to arrive.

The 1920s and 1930s saw a marked upsurge in people wanting to quit the confines of built up areas in order to appreciate rural England. Although London's tramways were considered an essentially urban creation, they did figure in the contemporary literature describing walks in the countryside.

London's Country. A Guide by Road, Stream and Fieldpath was published by London's Underground at Electric Railway House, Broadway, Westminster, SW1; it ran to several editions. It was divided into two separate handbooks – one for north of the Thames and the other for south of the river – and it concentrated mainly on the role buses could play in helping to explore the countryside. The MET did get a mention in a chapter detailing a journey out to Watford via Canons Park.

Barnet was also another destination featured in the book. We are told that:

The tramway route from Tally Ho Corner, at the junction of Ballards Lane and High Road, passes through North Finchley to Whetstone and thence to Totteridge Lane, which leads off left to the village of Totteridge, on high ground (410 feet), on the Hertfordshire-Middlesex border, about a mile away. The village commands fine views from its eminence and has a curious 18th century church with a huge yew tree beside it. Other objects of interest are the village pound and the Orange Tree inn . . . From Totteridge Lane it is a run of some two miles to the tramway terminus at High Barnet.

At the end of *London's Country* was a two page section laying out the direct and indirect ways of reaching Barnet, Edgware, Enfield, Waltham Cross, Hounslow and Uxbridge by tram. Although this was useful information, one is left with the impression that the three Combine tramway companies only had a minor role to play in the outdoor excursion trade. Ironically, it was that bastion of municipal trading and competitor to the Combine's tubes and buses, the London County Council Tramways, which really succeeded in popularising those joint MET/LCC services that ended on the fringes of the countryside. Two stylish, well illustrated guidebooks, written by Charles G. Harper, spearheaded the County Council's campaign to encourage working people out into the fresh air of parks, gardens, leafy suburbs and villages. It was hoped that the two handbooks, produced with the approval of the LCC, would 'introduce to readers many unexplored avenues of pleasure'.

Round & About London by Tram – Volume 1. North of the Thames makes no apologies about promoting tramways as *the* most cost effective way of getting to know the capital's history and topography. The handbook, which contains 210 pages, could be purchased for sixpence (2.5p), whereas *London's Country* ran to 104 pages and was twice as expensive at one shilling. Free copies of *Round & About London by Tram* were sent to public libraries, schools and colleges, where they were used to plan journeys. Many folk in those days could not afford an annual holiday away from home. Cheap fares enabled families to ride for miles, and with Mr Harper's guide at their finger tips, those eager for knowledge would not be disappointed. Each North London tram service receives a section to itself, and within the text there are many hints and suggestions as to what to do and what to see. Services 19 and 69 from Tottenham Court Road to Tally Ho Corner and Barnet merit no fewer than thirteen pages of description plus diagrams, line drawings and photographic illustrations.

Further illustrated accounts cover service 21 to North Finchley and service 29 to Enfield, plus tram routes to Waltham Cross and to Alexandra Palace. This latter destination had been almost forgotten by the Combine's publicists, but for the LCC and Mr Harper a trip out on service 51 from Bloomsbury to Muswell Hill represents a value-for-money excursion. Potential travellers are advised that 'on Wednesdays, Saturdays and Sundays the Palace and the Park are crowded with visitors'.

There is little doubt as to the most modern form of transport featured in this view of Wood Green. Feltham car 347 stands out from the competition. One of the 500 series LCC E/I cars, working on service 29, is about to cross the junction outside the new tube station. *D. Jones Collection*

By the late 1920s passenger comfort on these journeys was assured. Renovated cars in the MET fleet and new Felthams, which could operate as far as Whetstone and Enfield, formed the backbone of the service. Many LCC tramcars working the North London joint services had also been upgraded, or Pullmanised, so that they could match their Metropolitan Electric sisters. It might have seemed that the trams had turned an important financial corner and that all was set fair for the future; however, storm clouds were gathering on the horizon.

There were a number of threats, not only to the Combine's tramways, but also to the other London municipal operators. According to official figures, the only tramway manager able to sleep at night was Mr Harvey of Ilford. He was obviously coping well in his little corner of Essex. As for all the rest – increasing deficits, old fashioned rolling stock that needed replacing, inflated prices for rails and trackwork components, and the continuing irritation of bus competition all conspired to furrow the collective brows of tramway operators.

A growing campaign to replace tramcars by motor buses was well under way. This situation was already a *fait accompli* in some parts of the country. The electric trolleybus was also gaining ground; it was especially popular because tramway electrical infrastructure – feeder cables, substations, traction standards, overhead equipment etc. – could be reused or modernised for the new vehicles. Also, trolleybuses were considered legally as a form of trackless tramway and therefore they were obliged to continue to offer workmen's fares.

Finally, serious moves were afoot to establish a capital wide transport board that would amalgamate all public transport providers (with the exception of the suburban lines of the Big Four railway companies) into one organisation. Many observers assumed that, since buses and tubes took the lion's share of the passenger traffic, these forms of transport would be given preference in any future transport board.

As a complete contrast to the Felthams running out of Finchley and Wood Green depots, car 60 has survived almost three decades virtually unaltered. The long term use of antiquated rolling stock gave ammunition to the anti-tram lobby.

Car 42 and this interlaced track in Station Road, Harlesden, both qualify as relics from the beginning of the system. At peak times trams had to wait for the right of way to traverse this section, thus causing hold-ups for other road users. In fairness to the MET almost all of the routes had been constructed as double track.
D. Jones Collection

The MET, with C.J. Spencer at the helm, appeared to be bucking the trend; indeed, much of the tramway side of the Combine seemed to be prospering. However, the parlous state of the London United was an ever present concern and the future of the routes in the Kingston area continued to occupy the thoughts of the General Manager. An experiment with one man operated single deckers had fizzled out and the Combine was now faced with a large reconstruction bill for new tracks and rolling stock. On the surface, all the problems in West Middlesex were in marked contrast to what was happening on the MET. An official statement, issued by the board in April 1929, seemed to fly in the face of the critics:

During the past few years the tramway facilities of the metropolis have undergone marked improvement through the construction of short lengths of track to connect contiguous lines or to bridge gaps that existed between terminals of different systems. By such means the distances covered by individual services have been more than doubled. Two connections of the nature mentioned are about to be made on the MET, one at Horn Lane, Acton, where the MET lines converge on those of the LUT; and the other near Tally Ho Corner at Finchley, where the line coming up from Wood Green, via Bounds Green and New Southgate, will be extended from Woodhouse Road, across the Highgate Road and through Hilton Road to the Golders Green–Barnet line.

These connections will greatly extend the scope for working through services, as in the first named case a continuous line of tramway will be provided between Edgware and Uxbridge, via Cricklewood, Willesden, Acton, Ealing, Hanwell and Hayes; and in the other case, cars from Wood Green, etc., can be worked through to Golders Green, Cricklewood and Paddington, or, for that matter, even to Uxbridge or Brentford. The places named are quoted merely to illustrate the potentialities of through running that arise from the construction of short connecting links.

As a matter of fact, there is already a single track connection between the MET and the LUT at Acton, but it is used merely for the passage of cars between the depots of the two systems and not for traffic purposes. The connection for traffic working entails a road widening. At both Acton and Finchley the work will be carried out by the Middlesex County Council.

For a third important improvement Parliamentary powers are about to be sought by the Middlesex County Council. This improvement would take the form of a connecting line (about a mile in length) between the Tottenham High Road at Seven Sisters and the terminus of the Walthamstow tramways in Ferry Lane, on the Essex side of the Lea. The course of this line would be by way of Broad Lane and Tottenham Hale, and the effect of its construction would be to provide a continuous line of tramways between Epping Forest, at Leyton and Walthamstow, and the various Central London terminals of the conjoined MET and LCC systems.

The MET was obviously enthusiastic and the Company certainly had not given up the ghost, when it came to tramway expansion plans. There were lucrative possibilities in these schemes. Through services operated by reconditioned cars had already proved a success with the travelling public on the MET/LCC joint routes. It was not totally in the realms of fantasy to imagine an Epping Forest to Uxbridge service, where the Metropolitan Electric and the London United could supply Felthams to run alongside the new bogie cars being ordered by Walthamstow. There was even speculation that Walthamstow might go the whole hog and order its own fleet of Felthams.

Sadly, only the improvement at North Finchley would ever see the light of day. The other links envisaged would later materialise in a different guise – they would be covered by electric traction in the form of LPTB trolleybuses.

Further good news for the MET was announced in August 1929, when it was revealed that Southbury Road had been improved. Contrary to rumours circulating among the staff that the 'chicken run' was about to breathe its last and be converted to buses, the route from Ponders End to Enfield Town suddenly came back from the dead. The opportunity was taken to replace the old tramway bracket arms, supporting the overhead, with new traction standards and span wire construction. Ironically, the new electrical equipment along Southbury Road would eventually go to waste, because this particular part of the MET system would later be replaced by motor buses and not by trolleybuses. However, all this was in the future; for the management of the MET in the late 1920s these improvements meant that it was then possible for top covered trams to use Southbury Road. This, in turn, opened up the prospect of running through services between Enfield and London via Edmonton and Tottenham.

The other side of the coin was that in January 1930 the Company made a suggestion to the Alexandra Palace Trustees that both routes be abandoned; however, the County Council was not too keen. This prompted an about-face on behalf of the MET, and the Company produced an improbable proposal for new tracks in Mayes Road, Wood Green plus a connecting line between the two Alexandra Palace termini. Nothing ever came of these ideas.

An interesting tramway staff meeting took place at Acton Depot on 29th January 1930. Mr H. Oliver read a paper called 'Electric Tramway Conditions in Suburban London, Past and Present' – the word 'future' did not figure in the title. After the

This picture presents an interesting comparison with the view of cars 320 and 330 used in the previous chapter. Type H cars 288 and 285 look dated, but were structurally sound. Modernisation, in the form of fitting driver's vestibules, was later attempted, but by the early 1930s the trolleybus was in the ascendant. Note the EIGHT WHEEL BRAKES message in the triangle. This was a device to warn motorists not to follow the tram too closely, because of the powerful braking systems employed by the electric vehicle. You can also see why members of staff were instructed not to stand between the tracks, when tramcars were passing one another!
LT Museum

lecture, a lively debate erupted amongst the assembled employees. Messrs Spencer and Mason acted as referees/chairmen as Motorman Mercer of Wood Green suggested mass scrapping of old cars and the fitting of driver's vestibules to the rest of the existing fleet. District Inspector Ray of the MET advocated closer co-operation with the LCC. In his opinion, this was vital in order to combat bus competition. Motorman Picton of the LUT disagreed with Mr Hardman of Manor House Offices, when the latter complained about the bunching of trams in service. Conductor Costa of Wood Green suggested that the issue of workmen's fares was wrongly regulated, and this provoked Conductor Mardell of Finchley to query his employer's attitude to running the tramways. Motorman Williams of Stonebridge Park Depot injected a practical note into the discussion by saying that vehicles should be dried after being washed – they picked up less grime that way. The forum was ended by the presentation of long service awards to selected employees.

Five days before the Acton meeting, the annual dinner for those of inspector rank and above took place at the Trocadero Restaurant. It was given by the directors of the MET, LUT and SMET. One of the leading lights of the Combine, Managing Director, Frank Pick, presided over the gathering; Lord Ashfield sent his apologies for his non appearance. General Manager Spencer gave a brief account of the Combine's recent activities and he remarked that the MET and the LUT had had their most disastrous year in 1925, but that matters had improved since then. Frank Pick's speech was more circumspect. He dwelt on the recent collaboration between the Government and the Combine to frame legislation for London's future transport board. Rather tellingly, he said that tramways suffered from lack of space on the highway and this had hindered progress.

The most efficient use of road space was also high on the agenda of the motoring lobby. This powerful and vocal group, backed by influential public figures, politicians, the Automobile Association, the RAC, town planners and car, bus and lorry manufacturers, had effectively seized the initiative in the decade after the First World War. Freeing Britain's towns and cities of obstructive trams with their fixed tracks (I quote) was one of the main aims of this powerful cabal.

The lobby's short term answers were championed for long term problems, and this desire for instant solutions has dogged the history of transport planning in the UK ever since. Very few people around 1930 had the skill or temerity to make an accurate prediction of what *might* actually happen. Individual voices forecasting traffic congestion, mass private car ownership, gridlock, lack of parking places, exhaust pollution leading to global warming and ugly multiple lane highways as blots on the landscape, would have surely been drowned out by the chorus of supporters of the internal combustion engine.

In this climate it was not surprising that the prevailing anti-tramway bias should find expression in two of the main recommendations of the 1931 Final Report of the Royal Commission on Transport. The popular press seized on the following statements:

No additional tramways should be constructed. Though no definite time limit can be laid down, they should gradually disappear.

For many newspaper people this was manna from heaven and the official death warrant on tramways was greeted with approval. Editors and proprietors of the popular press were only too aware of the lucrative advertising revenues to be gleaned from motor manufacturers and oil companies; it was in their interest to be on the side of the private motorist. The only important matter to be decided was how long it would take to complete the process of ripping up the hated tram tracks. As far as the Combine was concerned, there was no immediate reaction to the Royal Commission's prognostications. However, it was widely felt that both Lord Ashfield and Frank Pick had set their sights on a tramless future.

The crew of this Feltham car, depicted at Tally Ho Corner, North Finchley, are getting ready for the return trip to Holborn.

Already in the winter of 1929 plans were being formulated for the conversion to trolleybuses of some of the LUT lines. C.J. Spencer in his Bradford days had had experience of successfully introducing trackless vehicles to the West Yorkshire city. Now he was being asked to do the same in Wimbledon, Kingston and Twickenham. As a sop to the dwindling number of tramway advocates, several of the LUT's trunk services were retained. Felthams were allocated to LUT route 7 from Uxbridge to Shepherd's Bush, in anticipation of the relaying and repositioning of tracks on private right of way on the median strip of new dual carriageway roads.

The popularity of the new trolleybuses, which started in passenger service on 16th May 1931, was not lost on those Middlesex county councillors who had made the trek over to Twickenham. Here they could sample what many commentators considered to be the coming fashion in urban transport. As regards Spencer himself, some sources claim that he regarded the abandonment of tramways as inevitable, and indeed, there are grounds to believe that he and Lord Ashfield were of one mind when it came to trolleybus replacement of tram services. However, his strong performance in favour of the modern tramcar at the Annual Congress of the Tramways, Light Railways and Transport Association in 1932 rather belies the idea that he had forsaken his tramway roots. A more rational assessment of his stance in the final three years of the MET would indicate that he had adopted the 'horses for courses' philosophy. In his world there was a place for all three forms of transport – bus, tram, trolleybus – according to traffic needs.

One of the highlights for delegates at the congress was a guided tour of Finchley Depot. L.B. Hewitt, Chief Mechanical Engineer to the Combine's tramways, was charged with dispensing relevant information on the MET's latest developments. Mr Hewitt had already published his account of the depot's transformation in the May issue of the *Tramway & Railway World*. After having been suitably impressed by the facilities and the splendid turn out of Felthams, the party was whisked out to Finchley Road to inspect a quarter of a mile experimental section of horizontal catenary overhead wire suspension. C.J. Spencer, in a note to delegates, explained that 'this method of suspension reduces by half the number of poles in the street, and gives a straight and level-running trolley wire'.

The plaudits came thick and fast. G.F. Sinclair, Rolling Stock Superintendent LCC Tramways, remarked that there was little doubt that the depot layout at Finchley was probably the finest in the country. Ronald A. Fearnley, General Manager, Southend Corporation Transport, echoed the general sentiment of his fellow transport professionals, when he said that he was filled with admiration for the modernised Finchley Depot.

A visit to the LUT's Fulwell Depot was also arranged. Mr Spencer gave a film show followed by a talk entitled 'Tramcars and Trolleybuses'. In the published transcript of his lecture, Spencer gave a powerful argument for the introduction of trolleybuses to the LUT. He also remarked that the question of extensions for the trolleybus system was having careful consideration. He announced that research was continuing in the development of a trolleybus with a similar seating capacity to a modern tramcar. Once this had been achieved, the Combine would be ready to replace trams in 'some other districts'. Unfortunately, he did not specify which areas in the Combine's domain would be receiving the new vehicles.

Some MET staff might have been speculating that it was their turn next. The Company had already dipped its corporate toe into this particular water, when an

The new tramway loading islands at Turnpike Lane were a bold and imaginative concept. Unfortunately, this was a case of 'too little too late'. After the trams were replaced by buses they survived until the autumn of 1968. *LT Museum*

experimental trackless tram had been given a trial in the grounds of Hendon Works. This event took place back in September 1909. Nothing came of the idea of running trolleybuses from Golders Green Station to Hendon. Another fruitless scheme was promulgated in 1913. Parliamentary powers were obtained for a route from Ferry Lane, Walthamstow to Wood Green Depot via Broad Lane and West Green Road. One of the main reasons for the non-appearance of MET trolleybuses was that the technology of the early trackless vehicles was deemed too unreliable to cope with the demands of London traffic.

Another pressing topic of speculation was what form the unified transport board for London would take. It was now not a question of 'if' but 'when'. Frank Pick in his speech on the opening of the LUT's trolleybuses told local dignitaries that the Combine would only be running things for a 'few more months'. Obviously Lord Ashfield was keeping him up to speed on the political progress of the London Passenger Transport Board Bill. The Combine management, with the support of the Government, were well placed to dominate the new board.

Lord Ashfield again figured in the news when he addressed the AGM of the Combine on 25th February 1932. The world trade slump had hit takings; the effects of short time working and industrial unemployment were being felt even in the prosperous Home Counties. After summarising the recent situation vis-à-vis the LUT, he concentrated on the MET:

. . . 54 new tramcars were put into operation on the Metropolitan Electric Tramways system, but they are insufficient to influence appreciably the results for that company, for again it serves an area which is predominantly industrial in character and there-fore seriously affected by the spread of unemployment. The fact that during a year of falling traffic the Tramway Companies actually carried more passengers than in 1930 is testimony to the wisdom of the policy. We have also enlarged and rearranged one of our tramway depots in order to secure the economies to be obtained by modern equip-ment employed in a progressive manner. This has been successful and those of our staff responsible for the planning and execution of the work deserve all credit for it.

One deduces from this speech that the Chairman felt the modernisation programme and the introduction of the Felthams had succeeded in stemming the tide of tramway deficits. Although it seems to be stretching a point to describe the North London suburbs, through which the MET lines ran, as predominantly industrial, the loss of earnings due to the Depression seems to have made a genuine impact, especially on those tram routes serving the Hertford Road and Willesden areas.

In spite of the gloomy outlook for the national economy, the Combine was pressing ahead with its tube railway expansion plans. On 19th September 1932 the Piccadilly Line was extended from Finsbury Park to Arnos Grove. This, as intended, cut the number of passengers wishing to transfer from tube trains to trams at Finsbury Park. At the intermediate stations of Manor House and Turnpike Lane, state of the art interchange facilities with MET trams were constructed. From the booking hall beneath the road surface at Seven Sisters Road, Manor House, stairs led to two tramway loading islands. Each island was eighty feet (24.3 metres) long and was neatly laid out with seats and a canopy, so that intending passengers could wait under cover. A similar arrangement was constructed at Turnpike Lane, opposite the Wellington public house. Cars from Muswell Hill and Alexandra Palace West used the updated facility. The new loading islands received much praise from the travelling public and the technical press.

It was unfortunate that the Manor House and Turnpike Lane improvements provoked no action to construct a tramway interchange siding outside Golders Green Station. The simple expedient of allowing cars to terminate off the main highway would have relieved congestion at the station and the nearby crossroads. As it was, plans had been stymied since C.J.Spencer had first suggested a double track siding back in February 1924. Repeated objections from Hendon UDC had killed the original scheme and all subsequent proposals.

Car 279 is pictured at the Manor House loading islands. This type of layout had long been a feature of continental street planning, and it was disappointing that these traffic refuges, where passengers could board and alight safely, were not more widely used in the UK. Trams last ran here in 1939 and the facility was not used by the replacing trolleybuses. Total demolition followed in 1951.

By the time the *Tramway & Railway World* article, illustrating the tramway islands at Manor House, was published in the spring of 1933, it had already been agreed that the London Passenger Transport Board would take over, starting 1st July. In February the LPTB Bill had passed its third reading in the Commons and it duly received the Royal Assent on 13th April. Lord Ashfield of Southwell would move sideways from the Combine to head operations at the LPTB. His official view of the task facing him was reported in a speech he made to the Royal Society.

The Chairman of the Combine predicted a great future for underground railways. The prospect of buses operating over an enhanced and upgraded road system also appealed to him. As for the trams, no mention was made in his speech of the Felthams or the new LCC prototype car 1. He implied that the development of a high capacity trolleybus would mean the death knell for the tramcar in London. The leading article in the *TOT Staff Magazine* for May 1933 seemed to confirm this opinion. It described the Combine's latest trolleybus – a 74-seater which had just entered service with the LUT. Great things were predicted for the new vehicle.

The Metropolitan Electric Tramways Company celebrated its final day of existence on 30th June 1933. The enthusiasm generated by the arrival of modern trams was now muted. As the Felthams finished their runs and returned to Finchley Depot that evening, the weather was quiet, but along the corridors of 55 Broadway, SW1, the winds of change were now blowing full blast and the outlook for London's tramways was bleak.

Some of the atmospheric magic of the tramway era is conjured up by this night time shot of Wood Green Depot. Shortly before the end of rail traction, the building is populated by traditional tramcars and the more modern Felthams.

13. Extinction

Contemporary accounts of the inauguration of the London Passenger Transport Board on 1st July 1933 fail to mention any public celebrations. As far as we can ascertain, no church bells were rung to herald the new era. It simply wasn't that kind of event. The initial transition of power to the LPTB probably went entirely unnoticed by almost all of the travelling public. In several council chambers throughout the metropolitan area sighs of relief from the elected members greeted the fact that responsibility for municipally run tramways had finally been handed over to another organisation. Furthermore, the deficits, debts and loan repayments would now have to be sorted out by the staff at 55 Broadway, SW1 – the chosen headquarters of London Transport.

The Metropolitan Electric Tramways Company contributed to the LPTB a grand total of 316 cars plus just over fifty-three route miles of tramway. Employees of the MET seemed to have accepted the change with little or no reservations. They were quite aware that the status quo would be maintained, because barring something totally unforeseen taking place, the old Combine was set to become the new owners – with Lord Ashfield and Frank Pick still pulling the strings, it would be business as usual. The only real sticking point seemed to be what to do with the wealth of human talent that the new board had inherited. General Manger, C.J. Spencer, was allocated the post of Tramways Manager of the Northern and Western Areas of the LPTB. In reality Mr Spencer's domain encompassed the three former Combine tramways, plus the lines belonging to Croydon Corporation. His colleague, responsible for all ex-LCC lines in the South, East and Central areas and the rest of the municipals, was Theodore Eastaway Thomas, former General Manager LCC Tramways.

This division of labour on the tramways lasted barely a few weeks. There were rumours of discord between Spencer and Thomas. The former then resigned from his job, and in October 1933 began a new career as Resident Director with the Northmet Power Company. The *Tramway & Railway World* published a valedictory editorial:

On both the municipal and company sides of the industry, the withdrawal of Mr C.J. Spencer from his position under the London Transport Board will be regretted. Strenuous as his work in the Metropolis has been during the past fifteen years it must have brought him the satisfaction that accompanies the conscientious performance of duty. That pleasure must have been particularly keen in his case, for he not only succeeded in giving the London United and Metropolitan Electric Tramways the pride of place in possessing improved and novel rolling stock, but also brought the renaissance of the tramcar in the United Kingdom . . . Mr Spencer's transport life of thirty-five years in a career of fifty-eight years has been one of devoted service to his chiefs, to the employees serving under him, and to his confreres throughout the industry.

At Finsbury Park in the summer of 1933 it is probable that many of the commuters pictured here were not much fussed who ran London's tramways – so long as they all got home on time and in one piece. Type G car 233 has been fitted with a driver's windscreen at both ends. It will survive as LT car 2278 until scrapped in January 1939.
LT Museum

131

Right LT car 2239 (ex MET Type H car 307) is seen on a gloomy day in April 1934. The location is the tram terminus at the southern end of Hampstead Road by the junction with Euston Road and Tottenham Court Road. Already the planners at 55 Broadway, SW1 – the headquarters of London Transport – had this section of track earmarked for early conversion to trolleybuses. *LT Museum*

Below right People emerging from the tube station at Wood Green would be greeted with this sign. It was illuminated to show when trams were waiting at the terminus in Lordship Lane. It represents one example of the integrated transport policy of the Combine, which was continued by the new board. *LT Museum*

Below Another illuminated sign, just a few yards from Wood Green tube station, portrays an odd mixture of design styles. The top panel featuring the bar and circle has been replaced by London Transport, otherwise the sign remains as it was in MET days. *LT Museum*

It has been said that Spencer left the employ of the LPTB because he failed in his mission to convince the policy makers to retain trams on the trunk routes leading to central London. There may be some truth in this, but it seems more likely that he was about to throw his hat into the trolleybus ring, rather than sticking with his previously held belief that modern tramcars could hold their own against their competitors. Whatever the causes of his resignation, the fact remains that tramway abandonment became the order of the day. C.J. Spencer's brand new Felthams were set to have a very short career in North London.

At the Nags Head junction car 2219 (ex MET Type H car 287) swings into Seven Sisters Road, while ex LCC Class HR/2 car 139 heads for Moorgate. In the coming months this vista will be altered by a forest of trolleybus poles holding up an impressive mesh of overhead wires. At least the conduit tram tracks were unobtrusive.

First in line for conversion to trolleybuses were those tram routes which had remained virtually unaltered since they were constructed at the beginning of the twentieth century. Four wheel, open top or open balcony tramcars operating at slow speeds over a run down single track and loops layout stood out in the mid 1930s as anachronisms in the age of the streamliner. This made economic sense. It was argued that, the quicker the old trams were substituted by up-to-date comfortable trolleybuses, the better for increased fare receipts. Although none of the MET services fell into the aforementioned run down category, it must have come as a surprise to many tramway stalwarts when, on 23rd November 1933, London Transport's first tramway conversion Bill also targeted a substantial section of former MET routes. All the western half of the system from Edgware Road to Acton, Sudbury and Paddington was going to be sacrificed, together with the complete route 29 from Enfield to Euston, and part of route 21 from North Finchley to Wood Green.

The early introduction of trolleybuses to North Finchley might have seemed strange bearing in mind the money and effort being expended to modernise the track layout at that location. The new road scheme at Tally Ho Corner included a gyratory system with provision for a tramway station in Old Nether Street. Partly opened in January 1935, all tramlines were ready for service from 24th February.

The LPTB must have been convinced of the crowd carrying potential of their new trolleybuses. They would have to cope with an upsurge of traffic, as the country came out of the industrial slump; this situation promised greater fare revenues on the one hand, but increased congestion at peak times on the other.

The *TOT Staff Magazine* had now metamorphosed into *Pennyfare*, and in the issue for February 1934 part of the task facing the tramway replacement vehicles was set out. It was reported that around two and a half million people annually used the Manor House loading islands, which channelled passengers between the trams and the tube trains on the Piccadilly Line. Some 2,218 people were counted on one day at the Turnpike Lane interchange. At Wood Green and Bounds Green passenger figures for those transferring from tube to tram were also impressive.

During the months before the changeover the trams were not neglected. Ex-MET vehicles received the new London Transport livery and their LT fleet numbers. The well known gold LONDON TRANSPORT transfer began to appear on the waist panels of the trams from May 1934. Progress was patchy with some of the older Company cars, which were destined to be withdrawn from service before they were completely repainted. Prior to September 1934 a total of twelve MET Type B cars were scrapped. On the credit side, the works at Hendon continued its maintenance and overhaul schedule.

Some MET route numbers, which duplicated LCC services south of the Thames, were changed to avoid confusion among the travelling public. Details can be found in the Appendix on Routes and Services. This change took place on 3rd October, but those former MET routes in West London that had been earmarked for early trolley-bus conversion did not take part in this renumbering scheme.

Not only the *TOT Staff Magazine* had been renamed; from 18th January 1934, the *Tramway & Railway World* was reborn as the *Transport World*. This was obviously a tacit acknowledgement of the fact that tramways were no longer in the ascendant. In the edition for 13th December 1934 a leading article, illustrated with an official London Transport map, described further plans for what remained of the MET. The section between Cricklewood and North Finchley was pencilled in for conversion to trolleybuses, as were tram routes along the eastern half of Severn Sisters Road, along Lordship Lane and Bruce Grove, and from the Wellington to Muswell Hill. The lines from Priory Road, Muswell Hill to Alexandra Palace West, and from Wood Green to Alexandra Palace East via Station Road were unlikely to be included in the trolleybus scheme and were classified as tramway routes to be abandoned.

The Paddington terminus of the Harrow Road route was just short of the neighbouring Edgware Road. Car 2320 actually started life as a member of the London United fleet. In a former existence it was Type T car 303. Some of the better West London cars were caught up in a rolling stock reshuffle, when the old open toppers were sent for scrap.

Car 2279 (ex MET Type G car 234) still looks good for a few more years' service as it waits at Turnpike Lane. *A.B. Cross*

The decision to dispense with the Ally Pally Bang Bangs must have come as no surprise to staff and public alike. However, it was not a foregone conclusion that the former MET Type E cars would be replaced by motor buses. Talks between London Transport and the Alexandra Park Trustees took place on 28th December 1934, and the idea was mooted of a through trolleybus service across the Park. Single deck vehicles would have been needed to pass under the low railway bridges on the approaches to the palace. As it was, the Trustees were unwilling to stump up the cash to subsidise the service; hence the decision makers at 55 Broadway balked at the idea of maintaining electric traction on these routes. Unfortunately, this meant that Londoners would never have the chance of riding on a G class single deck trolleybus.

In the first months of 1935 the trolleybus bandwagon started rolling in earnest. Contracts had been signed for the reconstruction work needed at tram depots to make them suitable for their new trackless inmates. Priority was given to the repositioning of some roof support columns at Hendon Works and Finchley Depot, and to the covering of maintenance pits between the tram rails. Out on the streets overhead wiring gangs were busy erecting new traction standards. London Transport was not obliged to skimp when making the conversion from trams to trolleybuses. Unlike some provincial towns, it was anathema for LT to recycle warn out electrical equipment or to adopt a range of ingenious techniques to strengthen former tramway traction standards. The job in the capital had to be executed to the highest possible level.

Extra traction standards have been planted at the terminus of route 45 in Cricklewood. Under the watchful eye of an inspector, car 2253 (ex MET Type H car 82) reverses on the crossover with the intention of continuing to North Finchley. The driver of the 63 bus will have to allow for the 'swing' of the tram, if he is to pass safely on the inside.

This desire for excellence was infectious. In early 1936, by the time the LT Tram Map had been retitled Trolleybus and Tram Map, many of the former MET staff were actively looking forward to the new vehicles. Some of this sentiment may have sounded distinctly ungrateful. Most motormen had to stand whilst they drove; only the Felthams had separate cabs and seats for the driver. Even some Feltham motormen were rumoured to find the arrangements in the cabs cramped and the driver's seat uncomfortable. They were looking forward to more leg room in a trolleybus cab. The publicity department at 55 Broadway fuelled the trackless revolution; they encouraged the travelling public to regard the trolleybuses as a marked improvement over what went before. The new vehicles were portrayed as the height of 1930s style and comfort. The distinctive sounds of the tramcar – steel wheels on steel rails – were to be replaced by the barely audible purr of the trolleybus. For those living on a tram route, this outbreak of silence after the conversion was a wonder to behold.

On 5th April 1936, trolleybus route 660 began operation over former LUT tracks between Acton and Hammersmith. The closing of Hendon Works for tramcar maintenance in April 1936 marked the beginning of the end of trams on the Edgware Road. On 5th July 1936 new route 666 ousted railbound vehicles on service 66 Canons Park to Acton. The opportunity was taken to extend the 666 from Acton to Hammersmith. Tram route 64 Edgware to Paddington was set to coexist with the trolleybuses for a few weeks longer. Tramlines north of Edgware as far as Canons Park were abandoned and it was not until almost two years later that this short section was wired for trolleybuses. Away from the hurly-burly of new routes and vehicles, the Hampstead Boundary spur at Childs Hill passed away almost unnoticed. It was officially declared *hors de combat* on 5th May 1936.

A member of the LT staff seems to have found a spot to rest his legs in High Street, Harlesden. Above his head is one of the new tram and trolleybus stop signs. Class C/2 trolleybus 271 is working route 666 to Edgware. For obvious reasons many superstitious folk hereabouts would never use this trolleybus route! In the foreground there is indeed evidence that many tram crews were bedevilled by derailments at this junction. Score marks in the road surface tell their own story. *D. Jones Collection*

On Southbury Road, at Enfield terminus, we witness a characteristic moment of tramway life. The conductor of car 2182 has swung the pole and placed it on the wire. After this, he will clamber on board, give two bells to the driver and then look out for following traffic, as the tram takes the crossover in front of incoming car 1064. The replacing motor buses will be positively dull in comparison. *W.A. Camwell/ National Tramway Museum*

The next casualties were tram route 45 Whetstone, Totteridge Lane to Cricklewood and route 60 Tally Ho Corner to Paddington. They both ceased on 1st August 1936. New trolleybus route 645 ran from Edgware to North Finchley and route 660 connected Hammersmith with North Finchley. The remaining trams in the area were only granted a couple of weeks' respite, before they also joined the queue for the scrapyard, which had now opened adjacent to Hendon Depot. Route 64, together with route 62 Sudbury to Paddington, perished on 22nd August. Tracks kept open for access to the scrap sidings at Hendon Depot were closed on 24th October 1936, thus finally bringing down the curtain on the MET's Western Division.

On the eastern side of the system trolleybus route 623 was inaugurated on 18th October 1936. The former territories of Walthamstow and the MET finally received their electric traction connection. The new trolleybus route ran from the Napier Arms, Woodford to Manor House via Walthamstow, Ferry Lane, Broad Lane and Seven Sisters Road. Less than a month later, with the abandonment of LUT route 7, all the former London United Felthams were driven south of the Thames to their new home in Streatham. Their MET sisters were now living on borrowed time.

Reports reaching London Transport suggested that the new trolleybus services were a success, with more people riding the tram replacement vehicles. The stage was now set for the total conversion of all the remaining ex-MET trunk routes. Inroads were also being made into the tram fleet. No fewer than 101 former Metropolitan Electric Tramways cars were consigned to the breakers' yard in the twenty-four months from January 1935 to December 1936. Losses included Poppy in November 1935. Centre entrance Feltham car 2168 (formerly MET car 331) was withdrawn from service and languished in store until sold to Sunderland in February 1937. Experimental Feltham car 2166 (MET car 320) met its end in October 1937,

to be followed in a matter of days by car 2255, Bluebell. On the credit side, only a handful of ex-MET cars were scrapped in 1937.

After the upheavals of the previous eighteen months, the year of 1937 turned out to be a quiet time for the ex-MET routes. However, rebuilding work continued unabated. *Pennyfare* for January 1937 carried the following notice:

Reconstruction of Wood Green tram depot for the accommodation of trolleybuses will begin shortly. The building is to be 550 feet long and 115 feet wide, and capable of housing 90 trolleybuses. Offices, staff rooms and a canteen will be provided in a new three-storey building on the north side of the depot.

In May the Coronation of King George VI took place. This national event turned out to be a major embarrassment for London Transport, because Central Bus staff went on strike from the first of the month and did not return to work until 28th May, by which time the tram and trolleybus department had been called upon to move record numbers of passengers. Cars from North London suburban termini worked from 3am on Coronation Day, 12th May, until 2am the following morning. They performed splendidly, transporting the crowds to and from the route of the Royal Procession.

Tram route 28, operating from Victoria to Harlesden, was partly replaced by trolleybuses on 12th September 1937 – the Clapham Junction to Victoria section remained tram operated. The last part of the old Harrow Road tramway from Scrubs Road junction now fell into disuse. In the October edition of *Pennyfare* a map was published, which showed in graphic form the true encroachment of the trolleybus on former MET territory. Readers were left in no doubt that the conversion programme was gathering momentum.

WHITBREAD'S ALE & STOUT

37 WOOD GREEN WOOD GREEN STATION ALEXANDRA PALACE EAST 37

LONDON TRANSPORT

2306

37 REPLACED BY FEB 21
...bus Route 241 daily between
...GREEN & ALEXANDRA PALACE

The printed notice on the rocker panel of this Type E car says it all. The old Ally Pally Bang Bangs are about to be axed in favour of a rather more mundane bus service. True to tradition, there appears to be absolutely no one about, except the photographer, to experience the end of this North London institution!
D.W.K. Jones/National Tramway Museum

There were to be no trolleybuses for Alexandra Palace. Tram routes 37 and 39 perished on 22nd February 1938; they were replaced by bus route 241. The last tram was car 2311; removal of the reserved sleeper tracks plus the reconstruction of a main road through the Alexandra Park took until the end of May. On the same day as the last cars left the Ally Pally, the final 51 departed Muswell Hill terminus in Priory Road, the service being temporarily curtailed at Wood Green. The Type E single deckers were hauled off to the scrapyard, which had been established on several sidings to the rear of Walthamstow Depot. It was in this melancholy place that the final acts of the MET would be played out in the weeks to come, as more and more cars reached the end of the line.

The revised 51 service terminating at Wood Green lasted less than two weeks, before the conversions of 5th March cut a large swathe through the remaining tram routes. The 19 from Barnet to Tottenham Court Road via Highgate was axed completely; journeys on bus route 134 were increased to cope with the extra demand. Route 9 from North Finchley to Moorgate became trolleybus 609; tram route 17 from Highgate to Farringdon Street metamorphosed into trolleybus routes 517/617, whose outer terminus became North Finchley. Feltham cars running on route 21 gave way to trolleybuses on routes 521/621. After withdrawal from service they were driven south to join their LUT sisters. As for the 51, it disappeared completely, through passengers being catered for by existing services. Route 71, which meandered around North London from Aldersgate to Aldgate, lost its Wood Green to Aldersgate section.

140

An extended article in the April edition of *Pennyfare* captured the atmosphere of the occasion. It ended with the following two paragraphs:

A Rousing Farewell . . . When the last tram left Barnet for Tally Ho Corner on March 5, so many people gathered to bid it farewell that special police had to control the crowds. Crowded with passengers, some of whom hung on the footboard or sat on the buffer, it was escorted to Wood Green depot by a cavalcade of motorists and cyclists, who played a fanfare on their horns and bells whenever it stopped. As it entered the depot the crowds of people sang "Auld Lang Syne".

Driver W.Lowe and Conductor F.Mardell, of Finchley depot, who took the first tram to Barnet thirty-one years ago, were in charge of the last tram, and the last passenger to leave the car was Mr Herbert Bee, who travelled on the first tram with the driver and the conductor. He still has the first ticket issued on this route – and now he has the last.

Mention of 'special police' brings to mind the fact that last night ceremonies were becoming more rowdy in nature. Many passengers wanted to take a nostalgic final ride, while some others wanted to push things a little further and were intent on stripping the tram bare of all its removable parts. This form of souvenir hunting verged on vandalism. One cannot help but note a certain grim irony in London Transport's complaints that trams were being wrecked by exuberant crowds, before the vehicles concerned could be sent off to the scrapyard to be cut up!

One vehicle that was not earmarked for an early demise was car 1, Bluebird, pride of the former LCC Tramways. It was hired by the recently formed Light Railway Transport League, a society devoted to tramway development, for an historic return journey traversing the capital from Waltham Cross to Purley. Car 1 clocked up a total mileage of 105 (169km) on the day. The fare for each passenger was five shillings (25p). The LRTL house journal, the *Modern Tramway*, takes up the story:

On the 15th May 1938, District Inspector Baker, an official of the London Passenger Transport Board, seated comfortably at the controls of the first LCC luxury tramcar, drove it from Waltham Cross in Herts to Purley in Surrey, and back again.

Yes, at 2 o'clock precisely, the familiar streamline design of London Transport's Number One Luxury Tramcar, slowed to a standstill in the narrow main street of Waltham Cross, Hertfordshire. And in the eyes of many onlookers we boarded the car with a feeling of possessive importance, not without some little excitement, for this product of man's ingenuity, this beautiful car with its inviting interior, was to be ours for the day.

The stretch of track that lies between Ponders End and Waltham Cross, and which has never seen a tramcar on Sunday for many years, was taken full advantage of. We literally flew. Down the road we skimmed, with the wind whistling past the ears of those members who stood on the platform, and who I suspect every now and then cast furtive envious glances at the chromium plated controls in "A" cabin.

Back in the work-a-day world, the last Felthams from Wood Green Depot were withdrawn on 8th May 1938, when routes 29, 39 and 41 disappeared from the streets. One of the replacement trolleybus routes was the 625, which worked from Woodford to Wood Green via Ferry Lane, The Hale, Chesnut Road, Bruce Grove and Lordship Lane. The third edition of the 1938 Trolleybus and Tram Map clarified the situation. On first glance at the map, only a rump of the former MET system

The conduit tracks ended at Manor House change pit. Car 2254 is about to continue its journey drawing power from the overhead trolley. Open windows on the top deck indicate that the weather on this summer's day in 1938 must have been warm. From the fresh condition of the paintwork, it would seem that this tram had recently been overhauled at Charlton Works.

remained. The Hertford Road services to Waltham Cross were still tram operated, as was the Southbury Road line from Ponders End to Enfield. Wood Green was reduced to route 71 from Aldgate; there were other connections to central London in the shape of route 27 from Edmonton Town Hall to Tottenham Court Road, route 49 from Edmonton to Liverpool Street Station, route 59 from Waltham Cross to Holborn and route 79 from Waltham Cross to Smithfield Market. The old MET wasn't dead yet, but it was on its last legs.

The beginning of the end came in two stages – on Saturday, 15th October 1938, and on Bonfire Night, 5th November 1938. The latter date was particularly appropriate, as many perfectly serviceable tramcars were set to go up in smoke. Car 2261 was the last ex-MET car to run on route 27. The *coup de grace* was administered on 5th February 1939, when route 71 was withdrawn. The final tram to leave Wood Green was car 1269. It was recorded that there were almost no 'festivities' at this sad event. The Metropolitan Electric Tramways Company had suffered a quiet and dignified death.

The Second World War interrupted London Transport's tramway replacement programme. When it resumed in 1950, diesel buses were the preferred option. Manor House could still be reached by tram until April 1952, when Kingsway Subway service 33 was axed. Car 199 is taking part in a farewell tour for tramway enthusiasts. *John Gillham*

After the closure of the last MET line, some of the late company's assets, in the shape of the Felthams, still had something to contribute to London's public transport network. They worked throughout the Second World War and defied the Blitz in south London. Former MET car 355, renumbered by London Transport as car 2099, was sent north to Leeds in the autumn of 1949. An extended trial was arranged, largely on the advice of Victor J.Matterface, who was a former MET employee and had left London Transport in April 1948 to take up an appointment as chief rolling stock engineer to Leeds City Transport. Following car 2099's success in Leeds, a price of £500 per tram was agreed and in August 1950 the mass migration north of the Felthams began. The 'London' trams proved popular with the travelling public in the West Yorkshire city and a total of 68 of the former LUT and MET vehicles had entered service by May 1952.

The end of the Leeds system came on 7th November 1959; ex-MET car 344 (as Leeds car 512) was one of the last trams in service. Most of the Felthams then ended up on a large funeral pyre; however, three members of Type UCC were rescued – one London United and two Metropolitan Electric vehicles. MET car 355 now resides at the London Transport Museum, Covent Garden. Car 341 undertook the long voyage to North America and it is now the property of the Seashore Trolley Museum, Kennebunkport, Maine.

Removal of redundant tramlines throughout the County of Middlesex was undertaken at a leisurely pace. Mr Jack Hall has given an account of his time as an employee of the contracting firm Gleesons. He was the only Englishman amongst the 25 Irishmen in the labouring gang that pulled up the rails in London Road, Enfield.

Lines of ex MET tramcars were stored behind Walthamstow Depot in 1938 on the scrap sidings. No further use could be found for these splendid cars and they were all broken up. *C. Carter*

144

The work of cutting up and carting away heavy lengths of steel tram track was extremely hard. During the 1939–1945 conflict the process of track removal was speeded up; the scrap value of the rails was greater, because metal could be recycled for the war effort. However, some roads carrying former tram routes simply received a covering layer of asphalt. In time this top surface wore away, exposing the rails like bleached bones of some extinct animal. Lengths of the former MET permanent way certainly survived on the Hertford Road and at other locations well into the 1950s.

What conclusions can we draw from the demise of the MET? Most Londoners in the 1930s felt that the trams had had their day; therefore, it is easy to assume that the system had little chance of survival and was doomed to extinction. If by some chance the Felthams and the North London trunk routes had continued beyond the Second World War, their replacement by buses would have followed in due course. UK public transport operators were so besotted with the internal combustion engine, that even large cities such as Liverpool and Glasgow, which had invested in the tramcar, dispensed with electric traction in the 1950s and early 1960s.

Trolleybuses were never viewed by London Transport as more than a one generation wonder. Although your present author has many pleasant memories of trolleybus rides over what was once the largest system in the world, the trackless vehicles were not a long term solution to increasing traffic congestion. Modern trams, as presently running on Croydon Tramlink, may eventually spread north of the Thames. If they were to return to the Great North Road and the Hertford Road, it is likely that construction gangs will unearth pieces of old rail – rusty remnants of the pioneering work of the Metropolitan Electric Tramways.

Relics of the MET system lingered on into the postwar era. In 1956 the road in the former tram station in North Finchley was resurfaced. The opportunity was taken to remove redundant tram rails. Temporary wiring for trolleybuses was erected over the adjacent carriageway.
R. Kingdom/LCC Tramways Trust

APPENDIX 1: DEPOTS

All transport operators need to keep their fleets in a secure place when vehicles are not in public service. It was a linguistic convention in London and elsewhere in the country that trams and trolleybuses were kept in *depots*, while motor buses were allocated to *garages*. Covered accommodation for the fleet was a necessity, especially in view of the vagaries of the British climate. However, large depot yards and outside sidings also had a role to play, especially when it came to emergency storage. Sometimes 'visiting trams' might find themselves out in the open overnight, before they were returned to their home depots in the morning. The core layout of MET depots, unlike those in the LCC area, did not include the installation of a traverser, which could shift trams sideways. An exception was to be found at Hendon Works, where two such devices coped with the marshalling of cars ready to use the maintenance bays. The rebuilt Finchley Depot was also equipped with a traverser.

Inevitably, because the MET's modernisation programme caught the imagination of the contemporary technical press, a detailed description of the new facilities at Finchley Depot has been included in the following list of the Company's premises.

Cars 2233 and 2261 at Edmonton Depot after it had been rebuilt in preparation for the arrival of trolleybuses. *H.B. Priestley*

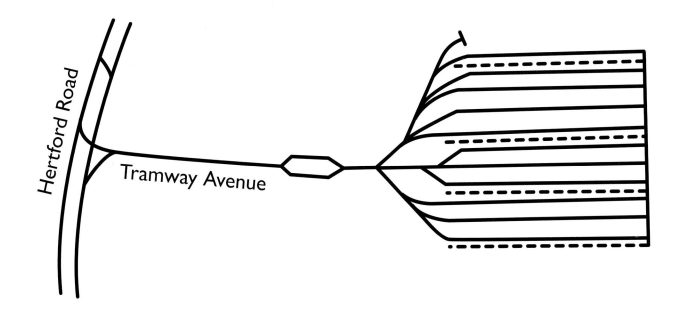

Edmonton Depot

This building was situated at the end of the appropriately named Tramway Avenue, Edmonton, N9. Construction work started in 1880 on a car shed and stables to accommodate the trams and horses of the North London Suburban Tramways Company. Fields and market gardens surrounded the new depot site, giving plenty of pasturage for the tram horses. A touch of modernity was added in 1885, when maintenance facilities were introduced for the company's new steam tram engines. However, the steamers were short lived and they were evicted in 1891, after which the horses returned for another spell.

On 26th November 1902, the Metropolitan Electric Tramways Company took possession of the site with a view to its reconstruction for electric traction. A sub-station was also built, and the whole depot was ready to receive its first cars from the late summer of 1904. Full operational status was reached in July of the next year, when connecting tracks to the rest of the system were electrified. A further extension of the main building in 1907 brought the capacity of the depot to 60 cars stabled on ten tracks.

In 1912 the depot was enlarged further and in December 1930 the MET purchased extra land, because it was thought that more space would be needed to accommodate Felthams. As it turned out, this plan was never fulfilled. A single line in Tramway Avenue branched into twelve depot roads on which cars were stabled. Aside from various store rooms and a sand dryer, the building once housed a traffic office, a staff mess room, a recreation room and accommodation for night staff.

Under the London Transport regime the depot was considered suitable for conversion to trolleybus operation. This was finally achieved in the autumn of 1938. Electric traction was maintained at the depot until July 1961, when diesel buses took over. The garage, which was designated EM for operational purposes, then survived until closure in February 1986. The whole building was subsequently demolished.

Layout of Edmonton Depot at the time tram operation came to an end there.

Finchley Depot

Built new for electric traction, the depot and connecting single line tramway in Woodberry Grove N12 opened for business on 7th June 1905. There was room for some sixty vehicles on fifteen depot roads. The 'tiny' fleet owned by Hertfordshire County Council was allocated here, and for this privilege the HCC paid Middlesex County Council an annual rent. The restricted access to the depot via a trailing crossover on Ballards Lane sometimes hampered traffic movements. Several proposals for a direct line to the Great North Road came to nought.

In view of the impending arrival of the Felthams, the whole building was extensively rebuilt in 1930–1931. Senior management officials were not only interested in streamlining cleaning and maintenance procedures, they were also well aware of the benefits in staff welfare that could be achieved. A leading article in the *Tramway & Railway World* for 10th December 1931 gave a detailed account of the impressive facilities on offer and the improvements in working conditions:

The transformation which has taken place has resulted in a tramway depot which will be taken as a model for present day ideas. By the wholesale introduction of labour saving equipment the operations of cleaning and inspecting tramcars are facilitated to a remarkable extent; the interior of the depot is kept clean and free from mess; the men can work in comfortable conditions, while provision has also been made for their welfare while waiting their turn to go on duty.

Extension was necessitated by the 100 new tramcars which have been put into service since January last by the MET and the London United Tramways, both of which are members of the Underground group of companies. These cars are 10 feet longer than the older cars they replaced, so additional shed accommodation was required.

A representative of the TRAMWAY & RAILWAY WORLD had the opportunity, with other press representatives, of inspecting Finchley Depot on 17th November. Mr C.J. Spencer, General Manager of the tramways of the Underground group, accompanied the party round the building, and was assisted in explaining the improvements by and other officials . . .

They wanted to get away from the old idea that a tramway depot was a miserable messy place where the men were destined to carry on their work in difficult and depressing conditions. They had arranged it so that dirt could be taken out without making a mess of the depot itself, as the litter, used tickets etc. was all removed from both saloons of the cars and the depot and was sucked up through pipes to a common point, where it was deposited in a container and then burned. The facilities for cleaning, washing, inspection and minor adjustments were such that the complete process took only about five and a half minutes, as the men who were previously scattered over the depot now concentrated on one spot.

One of the difficulties in a tramwayman's life, said Mr Spencer, was the split turn – when he had some time to spare and nowhere to spend it. To provide for that they had installed a very nice all-electric canteen, where a meal or a cup of tea could be obtained at cost price, a clubroom with billiard tables and other games, and a drying room where men coming in with wet clothes could have them dried . . .

Mr Spencer concluded his explanatory remarks by saying that the work showed that the demise of tramways was not yet in sight, and that his company would not have spent something like £25,000 on this scheme and bought a hundred new and costly cars if there was a prospect of a better system of transport.

The article then continues to describe the technical details of maintaining a clean and safe working environment. High pressure water hoses and the vacuum cleaning of tramcar interiors helped keep the fleet in tip-top condition, so that staff and the travelling public could have pride in their trams. Mechanical overhauls were also regularly scheduled in a light and airy setting, where staff could work comfortably in the cold winter months:

Each day a number of cars are placed in the overhaul section, on the basis that it is better to take the cars to the men rather than have the men moving from car to car about the depot. To facilitate this and give greater accessibility, sunk walkways have been provided between cars, also a transverse working pit with benches. In the pits there are two lamps on each side and one at the ends, which are prismatic design and give a brilliant light. The pits are heated by hot water pipes running along beneath the shed floor. The end wall for a height of 10 ft is finished in white glazed bricks and immediately above are windows running the entire length of the pits. By means of the traverser cars can be easily placed or removed as required . . .

A great improvement is also to be seen in the traffic and ticket offices, which have been rebuilt and redesigned. The traffic office has a new type of desk for the use of conductors when making up their cash, accommodation being provided for 24 men at one time. There is an open type cash counter with grill, fitted with four paying-in shutters. In the centre of the grill are two headway recorders, which register electrically the passing of cars on adjacent routes . . .

The article ends with a roundup of the enhanced staff facilities. We are told that the canteen has seats for 36 and that a variety of light refreshments are on offer. One shilling (5p) was the price charged for a complete, nutritious meal. There was also a water boiler so that tram crews and depot maintenance workers could make their own hot drinks.

Impressive though these improvements were, they could not withstand the trolleybus invasion. On 6th March 1938, tramway operation at Finchley Depot ceased. The trackless vehicles occupied the site until 2nd January 1962, when they too were consigned to the scrap yard. Bearing the garage code FY, the place hosted diesel buses until total closure on 4th December 1993.

Hendon Depot

Strictly speaking, this location was known as Hendon Depot *and* Works. The car sheds were situated on the Hendon side of Edgware Road, just north of Annesley Avenue, NW9, and were completed in November 1904. As planned, the place was to house a repair works and a motormen's school, as well as a fleet of some 32 trams on eight tracks. The original buildings were extended in 1912–1913 to include a bus garage for the new Tramways (MET) Omnibus Company fleet. This arrangement was short lived as the garage became surplus to requirements after the MET joined the Combine. Heavy machinery belonging to the Aircraft Manufacturing Company ousted the omnibuses just in time for the demands of the Great War to ensure full-time production of aviation components.

Hendon Depot yard was the venue for an experimental trolleybus route. On 25th September 1909 a trackless vehicle was put through its paces under a short internal circuit of wiring. A demonstration to delegates of the Municipal Tramways Association was arranged, and after this event the test circuit fell into disuse. It was removed in 1911.

From July 1915 to June 1919 maintenance work was also carried out at Hendon on LUT cars. Wartime shortages and this influx of LUT vehicles put a severe strain on both human and material resources, and the Works was hard pressed to keep up with demand. After the war General Manager Spencer was instrumental in a plan to use Hendon as the central overhaul facility for all three Combine tramways. The buildings were again enlarged to cope with a steady stream of trams coming from as far away as the Southmet in Croydon.

On site could be found a paint shop, a body shop and a lifting shop, plus all the equipment needed to recondition trucks, electric motors, axles and brake rigging. All this activity was scaled down during the trolleybus conversion programme of the mid 1930s. Trams ceased to be overhauled here from the end of April 1936. Hendon's life as an operational depot finished in August 1936, after which the connecting tracks to the Edgware Road were kept for old trams to be driven on to the scrap sidings. This sad activity continued into the autumn, after which the Edgware Road link was closed to trams on 24th October 1936.

In 1950 a London Transport decree that was supposed to avoid duplication of names, resulted in Hendon Works being reborn as Colindale Depot. It was later given the code CE. Trolleybus operation continued until 2nd January 1962; as in tram days, the site was used for scrapping redundant vehicles. It was never converted for diesel bus use.

Stonebridge Park Depot

This depot, built adjacent to the River Brent, was approached by two connecting tracks from Brentfield, Harrow Road, NW10. Tramway operation commenced on 10th October 1906. Although constructed for electric traction, the depot housed one horsecar for about five years. It was employed to enforce the Company's statutory rights over the Chippenham Road tramway. This line was not subsequently electrified and the solitary horse tram was disposed of.

The Stonebridge Park building, which contained twelve roads with accommodation for 48 trams, was extended in 1912. In 1924–1925 extra vehicles required for the substantial passenger traffic to and from the Empire Exhibition, Wembley were housed at Stonebridge Park. Due to the proximity of the River Brent, the land on which the depot was built was always liable to flooding. One such inundation occurred in 1928. The place was effectively put out of action and surplus tramcars had to be purloined and pressed into service as emergency offices.

In the new works programme of the mid 1930s the buildings were again extended and conversion for use by trolleybuses followed in July 1936. This form of transport then lasted until 2nd January 1962, when diesel buses took over. They occupied the site until August 1981, when the bus garage, coded SE, was closed down.

Stonebridge Park Depot forms the backdrop to this 1924 scene. Management and workers have turned out in front of car 65, which has been suitably decorated for service to the Empire Exhibition at Wembley.
LCC Tramways Trust

Wood Green Depot

Situated on the west side of High Road, Wood Green, N22, this depot was first built by the Metropolitan Tramways and Omnibus Company to house horse trams belonging to the North Metropolitan Tramways Company. The building opened in 1895 and was later reconstructed for electric traction. By the autumn of 1904 accommodation had been provided for sixty-two cars on seven stabling tracks. There were three single track connections to the main running line in Jolly Butchers Hill, High Road, Wood Green.

Further expansion of the depot occurred in 1908 and this brought the total number of trams under one roof to eighty-seven. Attached to the main running shed were a substation and several maintenance stores from which parts could be supplied for basic car overhauls. A yard, situated between the depot and Watson's Road, was used for stocks of permanent way materials. In 1920 a couple of sand dryers were added to equipment inventory; sand van 05 was then employed on missions to distribute bagged sand to other depots. Two mechanical tram washing machines were installed in 1927 and these labour saving devices speeded up the task of keeping the fleet clean.

In spite of all these improvements, the fabric of the building was extensively remodelled for future trolleybus operation. During the construction work two Type E single deckers used on the Alexandra Palace routes had to be evicted from the premises. They were found a temporary home on the siding adjacent to the former MET Manor House offices. The last trams left on 8th May 1938; their trolleybus replacements lasted until 7th November 1961, when they were shown the door. At the time of writing, Wood Green Garage (coded WN) still operates diesel buses.

For the tram aficionado, depots were fascinating places. In this corner of Wood Green two Felthams and a Type E single decker close off a space in front of planked over inspection pits. Various wheel and axle sets lie neglected next to the depot wall. Probably, they will never be used again. Their fate will be similar to that awaiting the 'Ally Pally Bang Bang' – a short trip to the scrapyard.
LT Museum

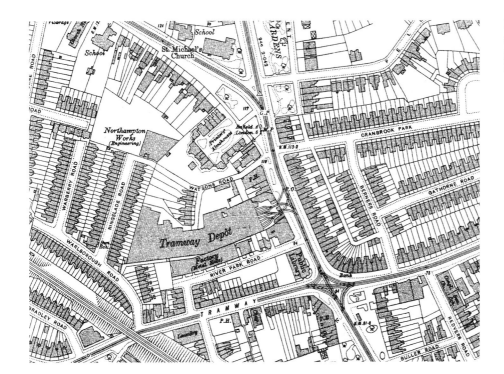

Layout of Wood Green tram depot and the wiring and track at the junction of Lordship Lane and High Road.

Manor House Offices

On the corner of Green Lanes and Seven Sisters Road, N4, some few yards north of the main road junction, the North Metropolitan Tramways Company erected a horse tram depot. Unfortunately, the layout of the building was deemed unsuitable for conversion to electric traction. A traffic office and a permanent way store, plus a yard full of overhead fittings, traction standards and feeder pillars, later occupied the site.

New offices appeared during rebuilding work in 1908–1910. They became the home for the MET's traffic and engineering personnel; to all intents and purposes, Manor House was considered as the company tramway HQ. Although the Combine subsequently transferred its administrative sections to 55, Broadway, SW1, the day-to-day running of the three Combine tramways was conducted from the Manor House offices. A siding led into the site from the southbound track in Green Lanes. It was constructed for works cars employed on engineering duties; it also provided a convenient temporary home for any stranded or incapacitated trams that had failed at the nearby junction.

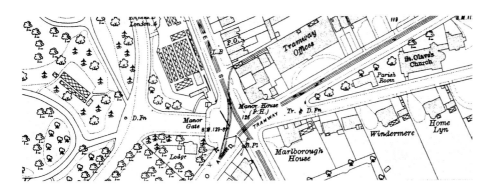

Manor House tramway offices.

APPENDIX 2: ROUTES

Potential passengers needed information on routes and services – where the tram was going and what the interval was between cars. A fare chart, normally displayed on the lower saloon bulkhead of each tramcar, would give an accurate indication of the cost of each journey. Armed with these facts, any traveller wishing to go from Point A to Point B by tram could be reasonably assured of arriving at his or her chosen destination.

Horse tramway operators in the London area had often allocated trams sporting a distinctive livery for a specific route, examples of which were yellow painted cars working from Finsbury Park to Moorgate via Upper Street, and brown painted cars working from Finsbury Park to Moorgate via Canonbury. This practice was not adopted by the MET. Electric trams were turned out in a uniform livery and were originally equipped with destination indicators and side route boards that listed the main places served by a particular line. Since advertising revenue was a useful source of income for the MET, the position of the three detachable side route boards was important. They had to be positioned away from the array of brightly coloured advertisements, so that people could read them.

The first electric services have already been described in the opening chapters. Right from the start of operations in the summer of 1904, there was always the possibility of turning a car short of its intended destination at a convenient crossover in the double track. A duty inspector might then ask passengers to transfer to the next vehicle following behind the car that had had its journey curtailed. Regular short workings were a feature of London tramway operations right up to the end of the system in July 1952. They were instituted to cope with varying traffic conditions, mechanical breakdowns, broken rails, wartime bomb damage or accidents that blocked the highway.

Some MET trams showed a combination of different coloured lights for route identification at night; however, precise information on this scheme has yet to be discovered. What is known, is that a system of route symbols was employed from 1906 up to around the outbreak of the First World War. These were gradually phased out with the introduction of route numbers from the summer of 1913. The major influence on the MET in adopting route numbers was the LCC. The London General Omnibus Company had been using them for some time, and it was part of Combine policy to standardise on this arrangement. In the first few years the Combine insisted that the suffix letter T be placed after each route number. The T presumably indicated a tram service!

In July 1913 the MET services, aside from joint LCC/MET routes, were as shown opposite:

Chichele Road, Cricklewood formed part of the important tramway link to the western suburbs of the Capital. As car 108 leaves the terminus, car 47 arrives at the compulsory tram stop in the shadow of the tower of the Congregational Church. This was one of the many places on the network where, during working hours, there was always a tram in sight.
Commercial postcard

10 Stamford Hill to Edmonton Town Hall

16 Stamford Hill to Waltham Cross

18 Stamford Hill to Finsbury Park via Wood Green

24 Finsbury Park to Waltham Cross

26 Ponders End to Enfield via Southbury Road

28 Finsbury Park to Muswell Hill

30 Turnpike Lane to Alexandra Palace West

32 Wood Green to Alexandra Palace East

34 Wood Green to North Finchley

36 Highgate Archway Tavern to North Finchley

38 Highgate Archway Tavern to Barnet

40 North Finchley to Cricklewood

42 Whetstone to Cricklewood

44 Barnet to Cricklewood

46 North Finchley to Golders Green

54 Willesden Green Station to Hendon Depot

56 Canons Park to Willesden Green Station

58 Paddington to Craven Park Junction

60 Paddington to Cricklewood

62 Paddington to Sudbury

64 Acton Market Place to Harlesden Jubilee Clock

66 Acton Market Place to Hendon Depot

The LCC Tramways Map & Guide to Car Services of November 1914 gives the following joint routes:

9 High Barnet to Moorgate. Through Fare 6d.

19 Tally Ho Corner, Finchley to Euston Road. 3½d.

21 Tally Ho Corner, Finchley to Holborn via Green Lanes. 4d.

29 Enfield to Euston Road. 5d.

31 Palmers Green to Euston Road. 3½d.

51 Muswell Hill to Southampton Row. 3d.

59 Edmonton Town Hall to Holborn. 6d.

79 Waltham Cross to Smithfield Market. 6d.

The Tramways Routes Map and Guide issued by the Combine in the summer of 1924 lists the following MET lines:

NORTHERN AND LONDON AREA

9 Barnet to Moorgate. Through Fare 10d. Journey Time 68 minutes.

19 Barnet to Euston Road. 9d. 58 mins.

21 North Finchley to Holborn. 8d. 56 mins.

26 Enfield to Ponders End. 1d. 7 mins.

27 Edmonton to Euston Road. 7d. 51 mins.

29 Enfield to Euston Road. 8d. 58 mins.

32 Alexandra Palace to Wood Green. 1d. 9 mins.

34 Alexandra Palace to The Wellington. 2d. 13 mins.

39 Waltham Cross to Liverpool Street. 11d. 70 mins.

49 Edmonton to Liverpool Street. 6d. 46 mins.

51 Muswell Hill to Bloomsbury. 6d. 45 mins.

53 Euston to Aldgate via Manor House. 6d. 62 mins.

59 Edmonton to Holborn. 8d. 49 mins.

69 North Finchley to Euston. 7d. 42 mins.

71 Wood Green to Aldgate via Tottenham. 7d. 52 mins.

79 Waltham Cross to Smithfield Market. 1/1d. 74 mins.

WESTERN AREA

30 Sudbury to Tooting. 9d. 86 mins.

40 North Finchley to Cricklewood. 5d. 29 mins.

42 Whetstone to Cricklewood. 6d. 37 mins.

46 North Finchley to Hampstead Boundary. 4d. 24 mins.

54 Hendon to Willesden Green Station. 3d. 21 mins.

58 Wembley to Paddington. 6d. 37 mins.

60 Barnet to Paddington. 1/2d. 88 mins.

62 Sudbury to Paddington. 7d. 46 mins.

66 Canons Park to Acton. 10d. 68 mins.

68 Sudbury to Acton. 6d. 38 mins.

The year after the LPTB took office, several former MET services were renumbered. Route 18 from Wood Green to Bruce Grove became 39A; route 26 from Ponders End to Enfield Town Station became 49A; route 32 from Wood Green to Alexandra Palace became 37; route 34 from Bruce Grove to Alexandra Palace became 39 and route 40 from Cricklewood to Whetstone became 45.

The London Transport list of tram routes for the winter of 1935 shows services operating over former MET tracks before the mass conversion to trolleybuses. Note that route 39 was worked in two sections. Route 28 only ran to Wembley Church on weekday rush hours. Cars on route 49 were extended from Edmonton to Enfield on weekday rush hours and Saturday afternoons. On Sundays, trams working route 79 operated between Enfield and Smithfield via Southbury Road. Through fares on the long routes 59, 71 and 79 cost just over one shilling (1/-), or five pence in modern currency.

9	North Finchley – Highgate – Moorgate. Service Interval 6–8 minutes. Journey Time 50 minutes. Through Fare 7d.
19	Barnet – Highgate – Tottenham Court Road. 6–8 mins. 54 mins. 8d.
21	North Finchley – Wood Green – Holborn. 4–5 mins. 60 mins. 9d.
27	Edmonton – Finsbury Park – Tottenham Court Road. 3–8 mins. 47 mins. 7d.
28	Victoria – Putney – Craven Park – Wembley Church. 5–8 mins. 87 mins. 9d.
29	Enfield – Finsbury Park – Tottenham Court Road. 4–6 mins. 58 mins. 9d.
37	Wood Green – Alexandra Palace. 5–8 mins. 9 mins. 1d.
39	Bruce Grove – Muswell Hill. 6–12 mins. 22 mins. 4d.
39	Wood Green (Wellington) – Alexandra Palace. 7–9 mins. 13 mins. 2d.
39A	Bruce Grove – Wood Green – Enfield. 8 mins. 34 mins. 6d.
41	Winchmore Hill – Manor House – Moorgate. 6 mins. 48 mins. 7d.
45	Whetstone (Totteridge Lane) – Cricklewood. 6–8 mins. 30 mins. 5d.
49	Enfield – Edmonton – Dalston – Liverpool Street. 6 mins. 61 mins. 6d.
49A	Enfield – Ponders End via Southbury Road. 6–8 mins. 6 mins. 1d.
51	Muswell Hill – Angel – Aldersgate. 8–12 mins. 42 mins. 6d.
53	Tottenham Court Road – Aldgate. 6 mins. 64 mins. 6d.
59	Waltham Cross – Kings Cross – Holborn. 6–8 mins. 75 mins. 1/-.
60	North Finchley – Paddington (Edgware Road). 6–8 mins. 64 mins. 6d.
62	Sudbury – Paddington (Edgware Road). 6–10 mins. 40 mins. 7d.
64	Edgware – Paddington (Edgware Road). 8 mins. 62 mins. 10d.
66	Canons Park – Hendon – Acton. 4–8 mins. 62 mins. 5d.
68	Acton – Harlesden – Craven Park. 2–8 mins. 17 mins. 3d.
71	Aldersgate – Wood Green – Aldgate. 6 mins. 95 mins. 1/1d.
79	Waltham Cross – Finsbury Park – Smithfield. 6–8 mins. 73 mins. 1/1d.

The first known MET map was published by Cook & Hammond in May 1903. Further examples of MET route maps appeared in 1910 and 1919–1920. Starting in May 1922, printed maps featuring the lines of the Combine's three tramways included a guide to tram services. Unfolded, the tram maps measured 14¾ins by 17¾ins (374mm by 451mm) and showed LUT, MET and SMET services plus certain joint LCC/MET routes that entered central London.

The standard of cartography was good; the printing and labelling of places served was clear and distinct. The series continued with Winter and Summer editions until 1932. On the reverse side of each map was a list of routes, fares and service intervals. Two 'General Information' sections carried handy snippets of information on children's fares, connections with the LGOC's bus services, lost property, luggage, dogs, special cars and parties, time tables and workpeople's return tickets.

Part of the attractive Combine map from 1932.

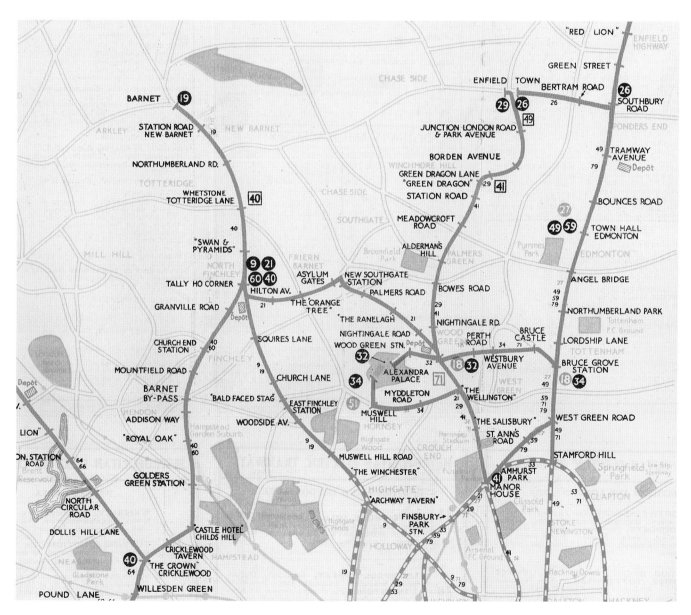

Appendix 3: Track Map

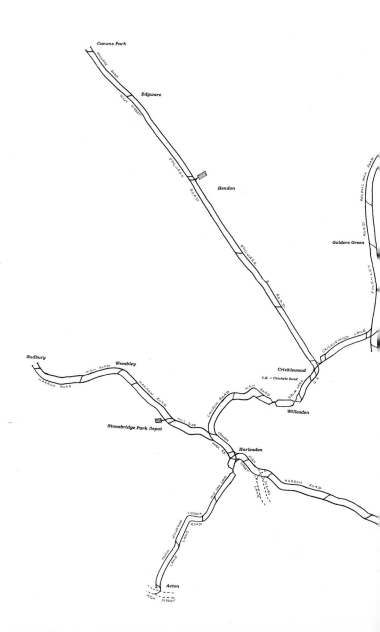

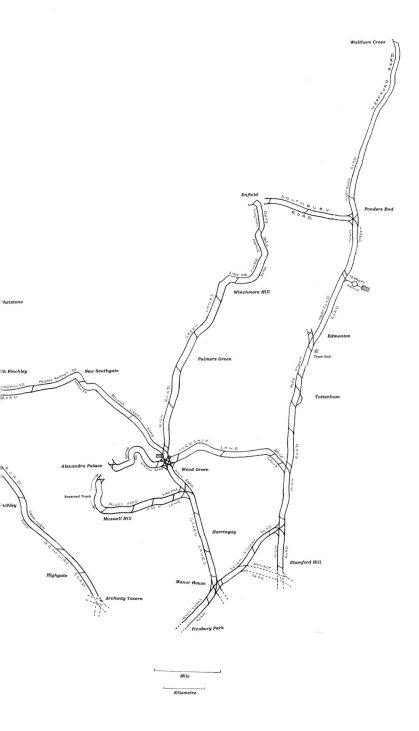

Waltham Cross

HERTFORD ROAD

Enfield

SOUTHBURY ROAD

Ponders End

HIGH STREET

TRAMWAY AVENUE

Whetstone

LODGE AVE.

Winchmore Hill

GREEN LANES

HERTFORD ROAD

Edmonton

Town Hall

North Finchley

FRIERN BARNET RD.

New Southgate

WOODHOUSE ROAD

BOUNDS GREEN ROAD

HIGH ROAD

PINKHAM

Palmers Green

FORE STREET

Tottenham

Alexandra Palace

LORDSHIP LANE

HIGH ROAD

BRUCE GROVE

HIGH ROAD

Reserved Track

STATION ROAD

Wood Green

Finchley

PRIORY ROAD

Muswell Hill

HIGH RD. LANE

TURNPIKE LANE

Harringay

GREEN LANES

Stamford Hill

Highgate

ARCHWAY ROAD

GREEN NORTH

Manor House

GREEN LANES ROAD

SEVEN SISTERS ROAD

HIGH ROAD

MANOR PARK

Archway Tavern

Finsbury Park

SEVEN SISTERS ROAD

Mile

Kilometre

159

BIBLIOGRAPHY

Mention has already been made of the three staff magazines. The *BET Gazette*, the *TOT Staff Magazine* and *Pennyfare* contain a wealth of information on working conditions, staff welfare and the daily life of London's transport employees. A list of other important reference works likely to be of interest to students of tramway operation in London was published in 2002 in the present author's earlier book, entitled *LCC Electric Tramways*. The two volume history of the Metropolitan Electric Tramways, written by C.S. Smeeton and published in 1984 and 1986, constitutes a comprehensive and detailed study of company tramway operation in the North London suburbs. The metropolitan volumes of *Tramway Classics*, published by Middleton Press and edited by the present author, present a fascinating picture history of all the MET lines.

The story of the Combine's tramways after incorporation into the LPTB can be followed in *London Transport Tramways* by E.R. Oakley and C.E. Holland, published by the London Tramways History Group in 1998. Time spent by the Felthams in Leeds has been described by J. Soper in *Leeds Transport (Volume III)*, published by the Leeds Transport Historical Society.

A good general overview of London's public transport can be found in *A History of London Transport* by T.C. Barker and Michael Robbins, which was published in two volumes by George Allen & Unwin Ltd for the London Transport Executive.

Ken Glazier's contribution to transport research in London has been immense, and on no account should readers miss consulting *The Battles of the General (London Buses 1918–1929)* and *The Last Years of the General (London Buses 1930–1933)*. Both works have been published by Capital Transport. Another expert in the field is Ken Blacker, and his two books entitled *The London Trolleybus, Volume 1, 1931–1945* and *Volume 2, 1946–1962* provide extensive information on the pre-war conversion programme and the subsequent history of the world's largest trolleybus system, many miles of which followed the routes of the former MET.